Rhyne's Guide to
FINANCIAL
PREPAREDNESS

Craig Rhyne

To Kemper and Betty –
Thankyou for your dedication
to good government and free
enterprise.   Craig Rhyne

**Expanded and updated
Rhyne's Guide to Barter (1995)
© January, 2018 by Craig W. Rhyne**

Published by:

**Washington Gold Exchange LLC
P.O. Box 368
Bellevue, WA 98009**

24-Hour Hotline (Leave a Message): (425) 522-3680
craig@washingtongoldexchange.com

**www.WashingtonGoldExchange.com
www.YouShouldBuyGold.com**

Dedication

This book is dedicated to my three children, my six grandchildren, and to the loving memory of my mother, Nelma. Nelma Wilhelmina Buswell outlived three wonderful husbands, including Alfred Avery Rhyne, Roy Edwin McCarthey, and Arthur William (Bill) Lofts. She was a lovely, charitable and wise Christian lady who worked hard as a wife, mother, and patriot.

Introduction

I AM CONVINCED that our country - and the entire world - will experience a financial meltdown that will bring more pain and suffering than did the "Great Depression." In the last year, in spite of hopes that President Donald Trump can stop it, I have concluded that United States debt and worldwide debt are insurmountable, and that we are beyond avoiding terrible consequences. Some see a continual "grinding down," without a ghastly overnight collapse. Others see an overnight collapse similar to the financial meltdown of 2008, but much worse. Only a return to the "gold standard" would preclude much pain ahead.

These thoughts have kept me up at night, and I've purchased many newsletters and books looking for answers and how to prepare. In the more than two dozen books I have purchased about preparing for natural and man-made disasters, books on survival, etc., I have found only a couple that discuss money. (None mentioned how one could use the old 90% silver coins for purchases. Only one book mentioned gold, but only dismissively.)

The truth of the matter is that precious metals maintain their values / purchasing power over time, while paper money does not. Recently, it came to me that I needed to update a book I wrote in 1995, with a focus on how to use silver and gold coins to trade for goods and services when the paper dollar fails. (My 1995 book had little about using gold and silver to barter with; the focus was the art of barter. Now, as we get closer to a "day of reckoning," I have been convinced of the need for an updated and expanded book.)

Bartering skills would be essential during a protracted emergency. But such skills can also be an important asset on a "normal" day-to-day basis. More and more people are turning to various types of trades in order to augment their buying power. So are many large companies, especially those who want to trade for goods from companies in countries lacking sound money. By simply bartering goods (or services), an individual can "do business" even when everyone else is waiting for the government to bail them out. Those waiting for the government often find all the good deals have vanished by the time they're ready to put their newly issued money on the table.

Almost any object, or even an idea, can be traded. The only limits on barter exchanges are the needs of the parties involved. Silver and gold coins and bars have been used for millennia, and they will continue to be used: to purchase everything from food to medical care and medicine, to buy property and pay for education, the list goes on and on. They are the ultimate forms of "real money," and we need to know how to use them in any case.

As with paper money, the value of objects being bartered will fluctuate. For example, you could buy a nice loaf of bread in 1970 for one quarter. Today, that loaf of bread can cost $3.50 to $5. But consider that an old pre-1965 90% silver quarter is now worth $3.40, about the same as one loaf of bread! The purchasing power of gold and silver will rise and fall according to supply and demand of the various goods and services (and the scarcity of gold and silver).

If you're only bartering for fun at a flea market or garage sale, the consequences will probably be minimal. But because we face tough economic times, I recommend you get serious. Many people discover harsh realities very late and are unprepared; ask anyone from a Third World country or an area that's had a recent revolution. Ask anyone who lived through the Great Depression about what it was like. Now the evidence is mounting that we face a terrible financial collapse that will make the 2007-2008 financial crisis seem like just a "warm-up" to what's ahead.

Craig W. Rhyne

$250,000 in gold, silver and platinum coins purchased two years ago. Now worth $297,000 (September, 2017). Green boxes are "monster boxes" containing 500 1 oz American Silver Eagle coins. (See Model Precious Metals Portfolios, Appendix B.)

Contents

What is De-Dollarization?

"**DE-DOLLARIZATION**" **IS THE** new term describing the accelerating abandonment of the U.S. dollar as the world's reserve currency. "The post-war Bretton Woods arrangements institutionalized the role of the US dollar as the main 'reserve currency,' and until the 1970s, about two-thirds of global GDP was anchored to the greenback." *World Economic Forum, 3/3/2017*

But this is changing fast. Increasingly, foreign governments are concerned about the burgeoning debt of the United States, which continues to create money and engage in massive deficit spending. They do not want to hold as much of their money in our Treasury Bills or Bonds. The BRICS nations [Brazil, Russia, India, China and South Africa], are now making deals between themselves with <u>payments in their currencies rather than with U.S. Dollars</u>. This is new, because for the last 70 years, foreign countries would use the "almighty dollar" to make payments to other foreign countries. They could depend on the sound dollar, which many said was "as good as gold." (They would hold huge reserves in dollars and convert their currency to U.S. dollars; then they would send those dollars to pay for goods from other countries.)

But with our enormous debt and deficit spending, countries see it better that they use the dollar less to make trades. The effect of this de-dollarization is higher prices for foreign goods…and accelerating price inflation. Unless we return to some form of "gold standard," a strong dollar will appear only in the rearview mirror.

Further, for many decades, foreign nations would purchase our debt instruments, Treasury Bonds and Bills. This helped keep interest rates low, but now they are reducing their ownership of these debt instruments. With less capital loaned to the United States, the cost of borrowing increases, and it becomes increasingly difficult to finance our debt. Thus, with de-dollarization, interest rates will rise, and each tick up will further imperil the federal budget.

Background: Lord John Maynard Keynes spread his economic theories from Great Britain around the world in the 1930s. His thinking infected most every business school in America, and it went like this: We can forever eliminate the boom and bust cycles by having a stronger central bank that tightly controls (manipulates) the supply of money and credit. Whenever the economy slows, just have the central bank (Federal Reserve) ease credit / lower all interest rates by reducing the "Discount Rate" charged by Federal Reserve for money lent to commercial banks. In this way, businesses that borrow money will have more access to loans, couples can more easily qualify to get home loans, etc., etc. This will result in more business activity and the economy will rebound.

Key to the theory was abandonment of gold and silver as backing to the currency. In 1924, Keynes said "the gold standard is already a barbarous relic." His attitude of "we can turn old thinking that says we need gold on its head because we are such enlightened economists" became dominant, and it lead to President Franklin Roosevelt calling in gold from American citizens April 5, 1933, an abandonment of America's "gold standard." (People received $20.67 per ounce for their gold; nine months later the government raised the official price to $35, thus cheating those who had previously turned in their gold. See a detailed explanation of this from the Mises Institute: https://mises.org/library/great-gold-robbery-1933.)

Eliminating the "gold standard" allowed all sorts of mischief, including a way to tax citizens *indirectly* through inflation. It was terribly easy for the government and the banks to create money and credit out of nothing when there was no requirement that it have one ounce of gold for every $20 it spent. The stage was set for amazingly huge expenditures on war materiel - including ongoing outposts around the world - and for the "welfare state" to follow. The Social Security act was passed in 1935, then Medicare and Medicaid in 1965. These entitlement programs promised stability and were natural developments of the increasingly broad interpretation of the "general welfare" clause in the U.S. Constitution.

The British Pound Sterling was the world's standard for money and the world's *"reserve currency"* until 1944. At the Bretton Woods (New Hampshire) conference in 1944, delegates from around the world formed the International Monetary Fund (IMF) and nations contributed tons of gold to establish it. Since the United States economy was the largest in the world and it contributed the most money and gold to the IMF, the United States dominated the process and the U.S. Dollar became the de facto "reserve currency of the world."

The tremendous expansion of government started by Roosevelt has continued through the years with little exception. President Johnson's "Great Society" caused the U.S. government budgets to rise and debt grew exponentially. Seeing this, several foreign governments increasingly demanded bars of gold (rather than holding our IOUs) in the 1960s. They wanted gold instead of a currency that was systematically losing its value due to inflation. As a result, President Richard Nixon issued an Executive Order in August, 1971, that stopped the gold drain from the Federal Reserve Bank vaults in New York. No longer was our government going to honor an "official gold price" of $42.22 per ounce. This was the final blow to the gold standard, allowing a free rein to those who wanted unlimited expansion of the money supply. Backing the dollar would only be the peoples' faith in the government and its credit. The "official gold price" became irrelevant. The "free market price of gold" was all that mattered, and gold quickly started moving up until the January 21, 1980 peak of $850.

Since then, the American populous (and its elected officials) has embraced an unprecedented growth in the size and scope of government. Instead of a "small" federal government devoted to national security and the rule of law, most Americans have gone along with "cradle to grave" (some say "womb to tomb") programs funded by taxing the rich (actually the large middle class) or by going into more debt. Increasingly, the federal government has expanded its reach to include a multitude of programs in order to tax one group to benefit another group.

So now we come to the 21st Century. *Very suddenly*, on Aug. 9, 2007, inter-bank lending locked up; the dollar was in *free-fall*; and credit completely FROZE here and around the world. The following year, Bear Stearns collapsed (March); Merrill Lynch and Lehman Brothers collapsed (Sept. 15); and the stock market crashed (Sept. 29, 2008). The Dow Jones Industrial Average had the biggest one-day drop in U.S. history; *Lehman* was the largest bankruptcy in U.S. history.

Hunter Lewis wrote in Where Keynes Went Wrong (Axios Press, 2011, pp. 148-9):

"In the years after Keynes's death, governments spent and spent, often citing Keynes as justification. By 2007, the year before the 2008 Financial Crash, the U.S. government had run up an official debt of just under $9 trillion but total liabilities of $67 trillion. This is almost five times U.S. gross domestic product (GDP) of $14 trillion. It was larger than the entire world's estimated GDP of $50 trillion, and almost as large as the estimated value of the world's real estate ($75 trillion) or the world's stock and bond markets ($100 trillion) as of that date. Most of the $67 trillion owed by the U.S. was off-budget and off-balance sheet, just as Keynes recommended. The Crash of 2008 then added as yet untold trillions to the total liabilities while reducing the asset values."

Meanwhile, Boobus Americanus does not think rationally about what has happened. Economic ignorance is rampant, and the politics of guilt and envy are pervasive, with cries by millions of unproductive people for more "social justice" (read this to mean 'forcibly take money from producers - higher taxes - and distribute it to others who have less"). The mantra of "tax the rich" and "make the 1% pay their fair share" is all the rage. This, in spite of the fact that 45% of all Americans pay no federal income tax at all! *"Marketwatch," 2/24/2016.* According to the National Taxpayers Union, the top 1% of taxpayers pay 39.04% of all federal income tax collected. The top 10% pay 70.59% of all federal income tax collected.

Our education system has failed us, with many teachers promoting progressivism and its father, socialism. We elect politicians who do not understand economics (who, themselves, do not know how to balance a checkbook, much less balance a federal budget). When our elected officials do meet to govern, they fail to address the sacred cows of Social Security,

Medicare and other unfunded liabilities which make the admitted $20 TRILLION federal debt small in comparison.

Since the global credit-collapse in 2008, the economy has been rocked by a series of violent after-shocks: the banking system came close to locking up again in Nov. 2011, Oct. 2014, and Aug. 2015. The Federal Reserve has kept the dollar system afloat by 'doubling down' on the excesses that led to the debt crisis.

"Global debt has hit a record high of $152 trillion, weighing down economic growth and adding to risks that recovery could turn into stagnation or even recession, the International Monetary Fund has warned." *The Telegraph, 10/5/2016.*

In 2008, we came close to a complete financial melt-down before the Federal Reserve took several steps to flood the economy with money and credit. You may recall the many programs launched, such as TARP (the Troubled Asset Relief Program), then three rounds of Quantitative Easing, Q1, Q2, and Q3. The U.S. economy has been in recession (not "recovery" as described by politicians) and our economy is in trouble. Attempts to raise interest rates by the Federal Reserve have been meager, because the economy has been weak in spite of the creation of so much money and credit.

The banks, the stock and bond brokers, and real estate firms have benefitted greatly from the wild expansion of credit (near zero interest rates) by the Federal Reserve. This system of "transfer payments" had been accelerating until the 2016 election of Donald Trump as our President. I pray that he will succeed in changing America's course. However, the Left dominates the news media and constantly rails against President Trump. We are witnessing millions of people of all ages adopting socialism in the name of "progressivism." Our forefathers, including our grandparents, would be shocked.

The dollar was re-valued *overnight* five times in our history: 1792, 1864, 1913, 1933, and 1971. It almost happened a sixth time in 2008. Now things are much worse than in 2008, and a war with North Korea is looking imminent. In such case, world leaders would not let such a terrible development "go to waste." It seems like perfect timing for a "re-set" of the world financial system, with Special Drawing Rights (the IMF's "SDR") replacing the U.S. dollar for international transactions.

I think the gridlock in Washington, D.C. belies the fact that the United States of America is bankrupt, as are some states, counties, and cities. Relatively few see what's happening, and warnings from the likes of me have fallen on deaf ears. While I've been wrong about the timing of a "re-set," I have been proven correct with regard to gold and silver holding value / purchasing power, while the dollar has steadily declined. When I first bought gold and silver, in 1970, gold was $40 per ounce and silver was $1.29. With gold now at $1,326 (9/1/2017), that means it has gained 3,315%. With silver currently fluctuating around $17.75 an ounce, that means silver has gained 1,375%!

Replacing the U.S. Dollar as the World's Reserve Currency

Consider the graph below depicting the 96% loss of purchasing power of the U.S. dollar since 1913. Note that the graph is current through 2010. Since then, the dollar has declined further, to about 3 cents compared to the 1913 dollar. The dollar is no longer "as good as gold," and nations around the world want to replace it with something that holds its value rather than hold their reserves in dollars.

The purchasing power of $1 from the time the Federal Reserve was established in 1913

1933: FDR suspends gold convertibility; makes gold illegal for U.S. citizens to own

The dollar has lost 96% of its value since 1913

1971: Nixon suspends Bretton Woods gold-exchange system

Source: BLS CPI Data

Regardless of your view on the viability of the dollar and whether we can somehow survive the debt bubble, we expect the dollar to lose its status as the "reserve currency of the world." This is not just speculation; nations are doing more and more business without using the dollar. Further, China and Russia have been buying gold while most Americans go about unconcerned, always hopeful that, magically, all will be fine.

"The Economist" magazine has told readers to expect a new world currency in 2018. *"Economist" magazine, January 9, 1988, Vol. 306, pp 9-10.*

We don't know the exact time, but I believe we are past the point of no return. Since 2008, Americans have been told bailouts were necessary to 'stimulate' the economy. Congress and the Federal Reserve have instituted unprecedented programs: Quantitative Easing [QEI, QEII, and QEIII - one TRILLION DOLLARS per year]; the "Stimulus Package;" "Operation Twist;" "Term Asset-Backed Securities Loan Facility" [TALF]; "Troubled Asset Relief Program" [TARP]; the *AIG* bailout; the *Chrysler* bailout; the *General Motors* bailout; Extended Unemployment Benefits, "Cash for Appliances," "Cash for Clunkers;" an $8,000 "Home-Buyer Tax Credit."

With artificially low interest rates, and an anemic "recovery," the Federal Reserve has few options left in its "tool box." Its actions to override the "free market" have resulted in terrible dislocations in the economy. If it raises interest rates too much, the stock market will crash and the interest owed on the now much higher federal debt will become unpayable without emergency actions that make our situation even worse.

For these reasons, I believe there will be a worldwide "reset" that will end in collapse of regular investments (cash, stocks, bonds, real estate, etc.). When this happens, good luck with money in your bank and pension accounts, and with Exchange Traded Funds (ETFs, where up to 40% of the money can be held in bonds - read the fine print). People will quickly learn why you must ask: "If you can't hold it in your hand, do you really own it?"

If you are considering precious metals as "portfolio insurance," the best way is to systematically convert 10% to 25% of your liquid assets into well-known gold, silver and possibly platinum coins. Think "portfolio insurance," not "investment." You will have protection from the coming dollar *"re-set"* if you have physical, tradable coins in your possession.

If I'm wrong about a sudden "re-set," and our elected officials change course and reverse the current trend to greater indebtedness, I will be happy. But I will continue to recommend clients hold an absolute minimum of 10% of their capital in "hard assets." In such a fiscal sanity scenario, I will view the stock market and real estate with less skepticism and will recommend them. But, unfortunately, Keynesian economics has dominated our schools and the federal government (and central banks) for almost 100 years. I seriously doubt this faulty thinking will be tossed into the "dustbin of history" without upheaval and great pain. Further, you would never cancel fire insurance on your home, even though the probability of a fire is low. The same applies to "portfolio insurance," which you should have by owning physical gold and silver coins and bars, regardless of your outlook for the future of our financial system.

Note: There are many economists and politicians who want to return to a "gold standard," where U.S. dollars would once again be convertible into ounces of gold. Some are saying this could come soon, and that gold would have be pegged at $10,000 per ounce to make it work. In any case, with the future of the dollar and world economic system in such a "pickle," it is prudent to convert a minimum of 10% of your assets - perhaps up to 25% - into physical precious metals.

"I Already Own Gold"

IN MY 45-YEAR experience in the precious metals field, I have heard many clients and prospects say they already have gold and silver. When I drill down, they reveal they own only stock in gold or silver mining companies. While I applaud their ownership of stocks, after admitting my bias because I don't sell stocks, I challenge them and point out that stocks are paper certificates representing shares of companies, not physical precious metals. They are "investments" that depend on many things, such as the ability of the management team of the company. Further, gold or silver stocks often act more like other non-precious metal stocks when there is a stock market crash.

Through the years, I have helped clients open gold or silver funded Individual Retirement Accounts (IRAs), where actual coins or bars are stored by the trustee's custodian on behalf of these clients. For those who are comfortable with coins and bars stored in far away locations, e.g., Delaware, please contact me to transfer your current IRA or open a new account with a precious metals-friendly trustee.

There are other ways to "own" precious metals, including Exchange Traded Funds (ETFs such as GLD and SLV) and precious metals royalty and "streaming" companies. My expertise is with actual, physical gold, silver, platinum and palladium coins, and rare coins. However, in the broad sense of the word "own," I have listed five major ways to do so below, with notes about the level of safety. By "safety" I refer to the least risk of loss, due to dependence on factors other than yourself, known as "counter-party risk" (third-party risk). The list starts with the most safe way down to the least safe.

1. <u>Owning actual bars and coins</u> and storing them in your own vault on your own premises. Further, you can diversify your storage to a private, non-bank facility, with the access limited to you (not a "pooled account") as the next best thing. Investments in physical gold do not have to be in the form of coins or bars. Gold is always a beautiful investment, particularly when it comes in the form of jewelry. However, calculating the value - based on the fineness / Karat and the aesthetic value - make jewelry less tradable and useful than coins and bars. (See Fineness / Karat Gold Values chart in Appendix H.)

2. <u>Gold, silver, platinum funded IRA account.</u> There are several trustees who will hold actual coins or bars of physical precious metals per the law passed in 1986 and expanded in 1997. Many coin and bullion dealers - including my company, Washington Gold Exchange LLC, can help you set up a new account (or transfer from an existing account) with an IRS approved trustee, such as Goldstar Trust, Equity Institutional, or New Direction IRA. This way of holding precious metals depends on the propriety of the Custodian that actually holds the coins on behalf of the Trustee on behalf of the owner of the IRA. Therefore, there is counter-party risk.

3. <u>Gold ETFs, Silver ETFs, Platinum ETFs, Palladium ETFs.</u> There are at least thirty Exchange Traded Funds have experts on their staffs buying and selling gold and other metals; they sell shares of their funds on the major exchanges. Most of them say they buy sufficient ounces of physical precious metals to cover all the dollars invested. However, there is risk in how the managers operate, and you need to read the fine print on their offering prospectuses, since some ETFs allow ownership of bonds with up to 40% of their funds. This increases one's risk exposure.

4. <u>Gold, silver, platinum mining stocks.</u> There are hundreds of mining companies around the world that sell shares on various stock exchanges. The biggest companies have mining op-

erations in various parts of the world; they are capitalized in the billions of dollars; and they are traded on the major stock exchanges. The shares of smaller capitalized mining companies trade on smaller exchanges and are often referred to as "penny stocks" because their share prices are under $5. When you buy shares of stock in a mining company, you get a certificate that guarantees you will be treated as other shareholders for dividends, etc., unless they are "preferred" shareholders. While stocks in mining companies can go up much faster than physical bullion (percentage wise), they can also decline much faster and act like non-precious metals stocks in a stock market retreat. Decidedly more risk than owning physical coins and bars - with counter-party risk - but appropriate to own for many people.

5. Precious metals royalty and 'streaming' companies. This fourth way to "own" precious metals is somewhat new, but offers an interesting and potentially very profitable way to participate in the inevitable bull market in precious metals. (Do you think our government will stop the printing presses and curtail spending? If you do, you should probably stop reading this book and watch TV.) The "streaming" companies issue common shares of stock and they have small management teams who constantly search for the best mining companies to invest in. Then, they provide cash to the chosen few companies in exchange for a "streaming" contract imposed on the assets of company. The contract stipulates that the mining company must pay the royalty / streaming company a certain portion of the precious metals ounces produced over the life of the mine. A fascinating and potentially very profitable way to "own" precious metals, albeit with more risk than owning physical coins and bars.

$100,000 in gold, silver and platinum coins purchased two years ago. Now worth $119,000 (September, 2017). Green box is a "monster box" containing 500 1 oz American Silver Eagle coins. (See Model Precious Metals Portfolios, Appendix B.)

Visit *RhynesGuide.com* to:

- *Setup a FREE 30-minute consultation with Craig Rhyne*
- *Sign up for monthly e-newsletters*
- *Order more books*
- *Access video reports*
- *Live chat: (206) 719-6368*

Gold and Silver Maintain Value Over the Long Term

I STARTED BUYING gold and silver in 1970 (when gold was $40 per ounce and silver was $1.29). Since that time, after hearing many economists, attending many financial conferences, and reading extensively, I realized how we have all been trained to be "investors." We are supposed to "buy low, then sell high" to make profits.

But the premise underlying this thinking is that the dollar is sound and that it maintains its purchasing power. Consider this example: If you bought a stock at $100 per share and it went to $110, that would be a 10% profit, right? However, would you really have a profit if the purchasing power of the dollar (when you sold the stock) had declined by 10%?

The obvious point is that the old "buy low, sell high" mentality must be constantly challenged. A change in paradigm is needed. Incontrovertibly, despite the sometimes scary volatility in the short-run, the prices of goods and services stay relatively stable IF YOU PRICE THEM IN TERMS OF OUNCES OF SILVER OR GOLD. The considerable research in Appendix C compares the prices of gold and silver to the prices of 41 common items, goods and services since 1970, then to their prices in 1990, 2010 and in August, 2017.

Please go to Appendix C and check it out. The text highlighted in yellow shows what the cost of the items was - and what it is now - in terms of gold and silver. For example, while the price of a loaf of bread was only 25 cents in 1970, and now it's $4 per loaf. In terms of silver, the cost for the same loaf of bread has stayed nearly the same: one old silver quarter! Why?

Because the old silver quarter is now worth $3.60! This is true of most all of the items, reflecting the fact that gold and silver have maintained their purchasing power over the last 47 years. (Stated another way: The dollar has lost purchasing power equal to the "gain" in precious metals.)

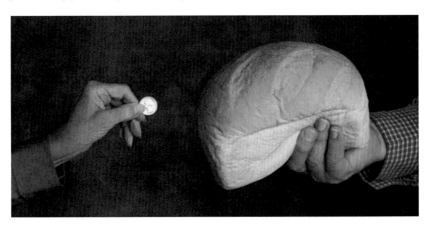

*You can still buy a nice loaf of bread with one quarter, as
long as the quarter is a pre-1965 90% silver quarter.*

The research proves the theory that gold and silver are excellent stores of value; consider these other examples from Appendix C: In 1970, a pound of red delicious apples was 15 cents. Today, these same apples cost $1.44. *Two old 90% silver dimes will buy you* <u>two</u> *pounds.* Hamburger was 70 cents a pound in 1970; today it's $5 a pound. But you can buy a pound of hamburger with just four old silver dimes because they are worth $4.80! A man's very nice wool suit was $40; today, a Hickey Freeman suit costs almost $1,600, about the same as an uncirculated old $20 Gold Piece. The average apartment cost $415 in 1970 (4 ounces of gold back then); today, the cost is $1,323 (about 1 ounce of gold). Health care back in 1970 was $355 per person per year; today it's $10,920. (In terms of ounces of gold, it's gone down from 10 ounces to 8 ounces.) Wages: The average wage is 8 times higher than in 1970. However, in terms of gold (and comparing gross income to the purchasing power of the dollar), wages have declined from 172 ounces gold to just 40 ounces!

These are just some of the examples from the research I did. In every case you can see that the purchasing power of the dollar - it's value - has declined terribly in terms of ounces of gold and silver. When you wrap your brain around how government inflates the supply of dollars and credit *and this is an insidious, indirect "tax,"* it is easy to understand why most Americans are distressed about the cost of living not keeping up with their incomes. The prices of goods and services keep increasing - as the purchasing power of the dollar steadily declines. Increasingly, the talk of "income inequality" fuels populist notions of going to the government for "solutions," such as raising the "minimum wage," which only accelerates price inflation. And instead of helping the poor, the result is layoffs and reduced working hours, not to mention businesses not hiring unskilled workers. The irony is that the government (through the Federal Reserve) created the problem in the first place by causing the loss of purchasing power of the dollar.

Solution: Gold and silver are good stores of value over time (in spite of their volatility), which is why I recommend you purchase gold and silver and convert at least 10% to 25% of your assets into physical coins and/or bars and take delivery of them.

The information provided in Appendix C can be used to come up with fair barter / exchange rates when using gold and silver in the event our financial system (and the dollar) collapses. There are no guarantees that the historical amounts of gold and silver needed to make a purchase will be the same in the future, and there will be terrible dislocations in the economy (e.g., compromised delivery by trucks or rail, for example) that will cause major shortages. For this reason, the quantities of gold or silver needed to make an exchange may change dramatically. However, this research is designed to help you establish a good basis and place to start so you can negotiate fair prices when bartering.

Those currently employed (with occasional raises) may not be alarmed about the declining purchasing power of the dollar. However, those who are retired - with income only from pension funds and Social Security - keep falling behind. And, ironically, they go to the government (clamoring for intervention) to solve their financial problems with more government handouts.

I am very cause oriented and have noticed this general trend over the years, verbalizing these concerns with the relatively few who will listen. It is not new; it is the story of governments all over the world and over all recorded history. It's just too hard for most of us to come to grips with the fact that our economic future is in great danger, and that the mighty United States of America could fall from its position of the greatest financial superpower.

I hope I'm wrong, and that we somehow muddle through our debt problems - and that there is no world-wide financial "re-set." Another way out of the mess (albeit with pain) would be returning to the gold standard. If we are fortunate to overcome what I believe to be insurmountable debt, acquiring physical precious metals is still an excellent thing to do.

Practical Recommendations

See Model Precious Metals Portfolios in Appendix B for general recommendations how to invest various amounts of money, from $2,500 to $250,000. Appendix A includes pictures of the various coins and bars that would work well in barter situations. The spot prices of gold, silver and platinum on September 1, 2017 were used in Appendix A and B to provide the coin prices. They were: Gold, $1,326 per Troy ounce; $17.75 for silver; and $1,009 for platinum. To get updated spot prices, go to the Washington Gold Exchange website: www.WashingtonGoldExchange.com.

I've taken great care listing the Best Coins for Bartering - with the very best coins listed first, as "Tier I and II." Then I supply a fairly complete list of other coins that are well known but are not of standard weights, plus platinum (Tiers III and IV).

Appendix D provides three excellent sources for emergency kits (in case of a man-made or natural disaster), emergency food reserves, "Bug-out" Kits, "First Aid Kits.," emergency power and water supplies and related items. In Appendix E you will find information about storing precious metals and other valuables. Finally, see Appendix F and G for a good list of resources, books and websites on many survival techniques.

Barter / Money Survival Skills

PEOPLE WHO'VE GROWN up in a society dependent on cash and credit often fare poorly when they have to barter. Many don't have any "horse-trading" skills or, worse yet, they fail to recognize the value of many items. When markets have been orderly, where they could depend on price tags, things are simple. But when the paper currency loses its purchasing power, price tags become less relevant, and knowing how to barter will be more useful than having a wad of cash or a nice, new credit card.

If you have the skills to barter and know how to keep a trade fair, you can continue to do business and "purchase" essentials for your family when the majority of those around you can barely get by. You can stave off intrusive government and not have to spend the last of your cash for necessities. In an economic emergency, whether in the aftermath of a natural disaster or due to poor government policy, the ability to barter could make the difference between living comfortably or losing everything you have. In severe situations, it could easily mean the difference between life and death.

If citizens are dependent on government currency, they'll be easily controlled by a government when the government has "legal tender" laws and anti-black market measures in place. Yet paper money is only a medium of exchange; it's only when direct barter (of goods for goods) is inefficient and the money is recognized to still have value that paper will work. That changes in emergencies when people stop worrying about buying luxuries and start focusing on the essentials for survival. Then they focus on gaining barter items that will hold their values --like silver and gold coins, bullets, or even cigarettes. These non-paper money goods become the new "coinage" in barter societies following financial collapse or other disasters. Just ask those who've dealt with hurricanes in the Gulf States, tsunamis or earthquakes.

The use of barter only in emergency situations is changing, however. Many people barter on a regular basis to avoid taxes. Others have discovered that cutting out the middle man, even if the trades are reported as "fair value" on tax forms, can save a lot of money. As more and more individuals become computerized and familiar with "online" services, such as Amazon, it seems likely that massive systems based on barter will eventually spring up.

Barter Skills in Emergencies

In many barter situations, the goods being exchanged can be thought of as "money." Items can be used as a medium of exchange and can be assigned a "standard value" - equal to the object that's being "purchased." In times of war, even cigarettes have been used as "money." However, there is much more flexibility and power to acquire what you want if you have a universally accepted "money" that allows for a variety of trades. For example, exchanging one old silver quarter for a loaf of bread would probably be easier than exchanging five pounds of oats for the bread.

Whether you're facing an economic emergency or a highly computerized society that no longer finds money essential for transactions, being a skilled trader can be a major asset. Such skills will make your supplies go farther and help you obtain good bargains, whether you're shopping for essentials or simply wanting some items that no one else can afford. Of course, bartering can't take place just anywhere. Whether in an economy based on money transactions or barter, there must be both a seller and a buyer.

If you're in an area where many people are dependent on the government (food stamps, other welfare programs, social security) or are otherwise unable to fend for themselves, you should think about securing your home from looters. Obviously, if people can't take care of themselves and there were an economic collapse, they would become desperate and the situation would not be good for you or your family.

In such situations, your first order of business is to leave, getting into an area where barter can be carried on with relative peace and safety without fear of interference by robbers. (See books / websites on this topic in Appendix F and G.) Additionally, you will want to develop a list of trustworthy people with whom you can barter confidently.

Like other skills, proficiency at bartering won't develop without practice. That means once you've read this book, you need to go to the nearest pawn shop, flea market, possibly even a gunshop, or other enterprise that will allow you to do some dickering. Learn how to do what was once called "horse trading" and hone your skills. You should start out small and then gradually work up to larger things as you become more confident and proficient. Before long you'll have the skills you need to be wheeling and dealing with the best of them w1ithout cash and without losing any value in your trades.

Cashless Society?

An important trend around the world is that modern technology is replacing the need for cash. Meanwhile, tax-hungry governments are happy to oblige. While most people think it's cool to pay for coffee - most anything - with their iPhones, the ominous outcome is that central banks move closer to having complete control of their financial affairs. Most people have little cash - leaving their money in a bank or other accounts which the government can monitor. Only a small percentage of people realize that if the government has complete control over their money, it means that same government has the power to tax these funds.

If an "economic emergency" were declared (such as with President Roosevelt), it is very possible that bank accounts would be given a "haircut." (This happened in 2013 in Cyprus when 48% of many bank balances were taken by the government.) Such a "bail-in" gives politicians the power to take money when it is in a government controlled bank.

It doesn't take a rocket scientist to see where I'm going with this… if you convert some of your cash now in a bank account into physical precious metals, you reduce your bank balance, thereby reducing the possibility of taking a "haircut" (or getting scalped) by a desperate government.

What Money?

Modern economists like to work with paper money and credit, ignoring the bartering that goes on all the time between individuals as well as with big corporations. In fact, such trades have become more common in recent years and are likely to continue to do so as various nations suffer monetary problems or tax cash transactions excessively. People and businesses do whatever they need to do to survive. In today's world economy, that sometimes means bartering.

Economists also like to avoid talking about how unstable economies can become. But modern-day Third World economies as well as those of major countries can suffer from run-away inflation or inflationary recessions that make the nation's cash almost worthless. Prosperous people and businesses that place their profits in paper currency soon discover their money is drastically losing purchasing power. In such situations, quickly exchanging money for goods and carrying on barter agreements are among the few tactics that will preserve wealth.

During such times, many individuals soon realize that money can be saved by holding no more than $10,000 in currency. Wise people start trading goods for goods and services and barter arrangements spring up. Such trading is frowned upon by the governments that created the market troubles in the first place; barter makes it harder for politicians to tax people. And economists don't like barter in such situations because it makes it hard for them to monitor human action. But for the individuals involved, barter can be a life saver that preserves or builds wealth.

Visit RhynesGuide.com to:

- *Setup a FREE 30-minute consultation with Craig Rhyne*
- *Sign up for monthly e-newsletters*
- *Order more books*
- *Access video reports*
- *Live chat: (206) 719-6368*

History of Barter and Money

DENISE RHYNE HAS written extensively about the history of money. To read her fascinating articles about money, including the background of many terms used today, go to her website: www.YouShouldBuyGold.com. You might particularly enjoy reading "Standardized Monetary Weights" under the "Silver & Gold" tab.

Additionally, the following article "Bartering Instead of Cash," is a fascinating account of barter in pre-industrial America, from this website: www.foodtimeline.org.

"Bartering (trading) goods and services in lieu of monetary payment was common in pre-industrial times. It was especially viable during periods of hardship and war. A farmer could barter grain and vegetables for a horse; a merchant could accept flour for tools, a cobbler could exchange a new pair of shoes for a winter coat. During the American Civil War, Southerners regularly bartered one food for another, or other goods for food. Salt was an especially precious commodity because in times preceding modern refrigeration, it was used for food curing and preservation. No salt meant no meat during the long months following traditional slaughtering periods (late fall).

"Bartering transactions are excluded from historic pricing data sets because there were no records published in the newspaper, captured by commercial markets, or reported by the government. Most accounts are anecdotal; found in letters, journals and diaries.

"Because of the depreciating value of the Confederate money, and the scarcity of specie, the primitive system of barter came to be a popular method of exchange late in the [civil] war. After early 1864 it was said that bartering had become the 'best mode of getting supplies, and those who… [had] things to barter fare well.' From 1864 until the end of the war, newspapers carried hundreds of notices of people willing to exchange one commodity for another.

"The following advertisement, which appeared in the Savannah *Republican*, was typical: 'I will barter salt from my salt factory for produce on the following terms: Salt, 50 pounds per bushel; 4 bushels of salt for 5 bushels of corn and peas; 1 bushel of salt for 5 pounds of lard or bacon; 2 bushels of salt for 7 pounds of sugar; 10 bushels of salt for a barrel of 'super' flour; 2 bushels of salt for 1 pr. of shoes.'

"The acceptance of foodstuffs in return for tuition or board in colleges and schools became general. Forsaking altogether monetary payments, farmers would load whatever they had to offer on a wagon or cart and take it around the countryside trying to exchange it for what they had not…One woman, once a lady of means, found it necessary to sell her $600 New Orleans-made bonnet. Instead of money, she took five turkeys in payment."

"Source: *Ersatz in the Confederacy: Shortages and Substitutes on the Southern Homefront*, 1952 facsimile edition, Mary Elizabeth Massey [University of South Carolina Press: Columbia] 1993 (p. 168)"

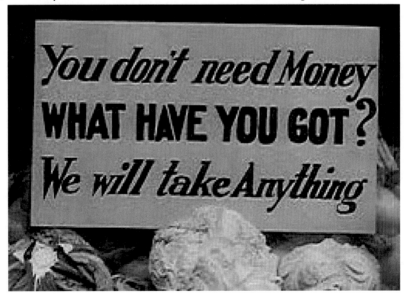

Financial System "Re-set"

WHAT HAS HAPPENED in other countries not only *can* happen in the US… it has before. The Great Depression forced many people to barter when money became scarce. Forty years later, President Carter's double-digit inflation in the 1970s nearly wrecked the economy. Of course, today's economists like to pretend that such potential disasters are under control in the US. "The Federal Reserve wouldn't let that happen," we are told. And yet these economists are often surprised or shocked when the economy goes in the opposite direction they've predicted, such as in 2007-2008.

In fact, the economy isn't fully understood and its stability is as much an illusion as anything else. As long as everyone believes the illusion, the economy is sound. But if Americans ever stop trusting the dollar and that the economy will be stable, a run-away depression or a destructive round of inflation could occur.

Mainstream (Keynesian] economists, who often incorrectly predict which direction the economy is headed, also like to portray a cash-based society (with the currency backed by physical gold or silver) as being very primitive. They advocate having central banks that control and expand credit and the money supply to stimulate the economy. The result is inflation of prices, ultimately destroying the currency's purchasing power.

In reality, a barter economy isn't all that unusual because cash, until 1933, was based on being equal to very discrete amounts of precious metals (gold and silver). In effect, when a person purchased a car or whatever with money, he was really trading gold and silver for the item. But when President Roosevelt called in gold (April 5, 1933) that all changed, and our government started printing money (and expanded credit), and our paper money no longer said "redeemable in gold or silver."

The government removed language on our paper money such as "gold certificate" or "silver certificate." These and other acts allowed the government to finance its redistribution schemes and pay for expansion of the state (with thousands of programs) and finance the military. Debt expansion, not limited to holdings of physical gold or silver, allowed government spending to grow without any limitation because it was not even restricted by the amount of taxes collected from the people. Thus, it can no longer be said that the "U.S. Dollar is as good as gold." And it gets worse by the day.

So, given that the dollar will continue to lose purchasing power, with the likelihood of collapse, you need to change your thinking from "buy low, sell high." That thinking no longer applies because it can only work if the underlying currency maintains its purchasing power (backed by gold). If purchasing power of the currency is maintained, the gains in the investments are real. But if the currency is constantly losing value, the investment "gain" is illusory if it is not greater than the loss of purchasing power of the dollar. Even worse, the artificial gain often causes people to be pushed into a higher tax bracket.

Clearly, with the failed Keynesians in control of world economies promoting unsustainable creation of money and credit, you need to protect your capital with a form of "monetary insurance." You can do this by converting at least 10%, possibly up to 25%, of your assets into physical precious metals. And learn to barter. As the collapse of a currency comes closer, it becomes increasingly apparent that trading goods and services for other items - or for gold and silver coins - is the best way to protect your family and allow you to weather most any natural or man-made disaster. (See Best Coins for Barter in Appendix A.)

Second Nature

Once you get used to the idea of bartering, you'll discover that it's almost second nature to you. In fact, you'll probably soon remember trades you engaged in as a child; baseball cards, toys, clothing, and what-have-you were traded for items you wanted. The big catch to bartering is that it's similar to conducting business with only 20-dollar bills (or perhaps 100-dollar bills). As long as you're negotiating for big ticket items, no problem. But when you need to trade for, say, one energy bar, you need items of less value than big bills. In this case, you could trade a couple eggs for the energy bar. The point is you want very tradeable items, divisible for small transactions.

You don't want to end up with a bunch of stuff you don't need, or huge lots, spending your barter items unwisely. Alternately, if you had some old, pre-1965 U.S. 90% silver dimes, currently selling for about $1.45, you could easily "barter" the one 90% silver dime for the energy bar!

Despite the potential awkwardness of barter when it comes to exchanging small items or services, it isn't all that hard if you're used to stretching your dollars. The difference is that items you barter probably won't have price tags on them. You and the person you're trading with have to decide if an hour of your time, the shirt your wife sewed, or whatever you're bartering is worth $2, $20, or $200 (or one old silver dime or a 1/10 oz gold coin, for example). Coming to agreement on values can make things a bit complex until all the parties involved get the hang of it.

The only catch to this, and one all traders must keep in mind, is that if something becomes too valuable or too scarce, people may figure out a way to do without it or make a substitute. For this reason, care must be taken not to "price yourself out of the market" by holding onto a valuable commodity for too long. This is especially important to remember during times of crisis or when you're bartering relatively expensive goods or services.

Just as there can be "runs" when speculators drive up the buying power of silver coins, so, too, can the apparent value of any barter item be driven up or down. Good barterers know this and employ their knowledge on a very localized scale to get better deals for themselves. They enhance the demand for their products while lowering the apparent demand for what they want in trade. (If you don't know what's going on, someone exploiting this technique can steal you blind -- and make you think you're getting the best part of the bargain.)

Hi-Tech Barter

When you're engaged in bartering, keep in mind that barter doesn't only entail the trading of goods. Information and services can also be bartered. If you have special talents or know-how that might be of use to another, those can be traded, too. The big plus of such barter services is that you can carry these talents around freely without fear of them being stolen by a thief or draconian government. For this reason, it pays to hone skills that might be employed to barter for goods that you need. The old saw about a doctor never starving is true; anyone with a valuable skill can always trade his services for necessities.

Barter has another plus over paper money in that you can mix goods and services in any way you like to make a trade work. Suppose, for example, that you need to trade for a milk cow or the services of a doctor. In such cases, you don't have to have just one thing to trade that's exactly worth the value of the services you need. Instead, you can trade a variety of objects. You might, for example, trade an old antique gold watch, a crate of vegetables from your garden, and the promise to do an hour's worth of plumbing in exchange for a cow or the doctor's baby delivery services. This ability to throw in various items in a trade - augmented with silver and gold coins, if needed - makes it possible to tailor your purchases to what you have on hand, and it also makes it possible to more or less cater to the needs of the person with whom you are trading.

The Failure of Government

When a government's money fails noticeably, people often use a common commodity to take the place of money. In such extreme circumstances, junk-silver pre-1965 dimes, quarters, half-dollars and silver dollars, gold coins (in many sizes), candy, cigarettes, cognac, or other small, universally recognized commodities become "money" useful as a medium for barter. Unlike the case with paper money, when the government dictates that everyone must use the coin of the realm (or else!), commodities that take the place of money can operate side by side. Thus, you might see people trading old coins, silver or gold bars, ammunition, and candy in various transactions and perhaps mixing the combinations in various barter deals. Other times you might see a large commodity bartered for a smaller one with the "balance" due paid with coins, cigarettes, chocolate, ammunition, and/or sugar in varying amounts to make the trade even.

Such economies present an opportunity to anyone who can manufacture goods that can be traded in place of money. Such people can, in effect, manufacture "barter money." If you can maneuver yourself into such an ideal position in a barter economy, you will be in the catbird's seat. For this reason you should give some thought now to learning to reload ammunition, for example. Being able to produce items for bartering would assure that you would be self-sufficient in the new culture that emerged until a new, stable government took over and the government money was dependable. If you don't have such talents, you will do fine if you have old silver coins. (There will be an "acceleration of information" as the economy worsens and devolves in a financial meltdown, and people will learn fast the value of silver and gold coins.)

"Making Money"

If you get into the barter money manufacturing business, e.g., producing packages of four cigarettes, don't invest too much time or money in the production. The marketplace is fickle and your market for any commodity is limited. Your "currency" may become almost valueless overnight or be replaced by another product. For example, you might be wise to purchase an inexpensive reloading press to make ammunition. But it may be a mistake to expand your business, buying more equipment and hiring more help; you would not want to saturate your market and lose the bargaining edge your product has. Barter economies, like paper money economies, run on supply and demand. If you produce too much of any product, even if it's being used for cash, it can quickly lose its value. If you invest extensively in producing such "barter cash" for a limited local market, you could lose your shirt.

That said, it would be good to learn some "old world" trades, such as how to do gunsmithing. However, in addition to developing a skill you can barter, or manufacturing "barter cash," you should own silver and gold coins and be diversified. The universal tradability of coins makes them superior to all other items or services in a barter situation.

Visit RhynesGuide.com to:

- *Setup a FREE 30-minute*
- *consultation with Craig Rhyne*
- *Signup for insightful e-newsletters*
- *Order more books*
- *Access video reports*
- *Live chat: (206) 719-6368*

Government Encroachment
& Violence

GOVERNMENTS DON'T TAKE kindly to barter. Currently, you're required to report barter on your tax forms. But figuring exactly how much you owe gets pretty iffy since you have to estimate the profit you made on the trade. And if you're only trading for something of like kind that's used in your business, then you don't have to report the trade at all. Needless to say, barter is currently something that the IRS prefers not to think about, but for which it will take you to task if you appear to be gaming the tax man with it.

During an economic emergency, governments normally create new paper money to replace the old, often offering exchange rates that basically cheat the owners of the old cash and cover up the destruction of the currency by the government. Throughout history, in the most severe economic conditions, many people have chosen not to use the new money, realizing that it could become worthless overnight with another "trade in" of the new currency for even newer currency. As this failure of people to trust the new money grows, a barter economy fills the void.

"Black Markets"

Governments don't like a barter economy since it limits their ability to tax money through the banking system - and it also cuts into a government's ability to control the people with such things as "capital controls." However, if the regular economy has collapsed, black markets will spring up where people engage in trading goods and services between themselves.

Thus, bartering would become a valuable way to survive and provide for your family - and small, tradable sizes of gold and silver coins and bars would provide great flexibility. Note that if the government were to create an emergency currency in enormous quantities, the best strategy would probably be to spend it quickly (though not recklessly) and then switch to bartering.

In a black market, businesses often hide merchandise, keeping it for barter rather than making it available for sale for the government's currency (which may legally have to be accepted in trade). Another ploy used is to raise the prices of goods to keep people from purchasing them. Either way, you'll discover that if you can barter for such a business's goods, merchants may have a lot more merchandise available in back rooms than they do on their display shelves. For this reason, barter can give you an important edge, especially when essential supplies (including food) appear to be in short supply but are actually hidden and out of sight from cash-paying customers.

In addition to helping you deal with worthless government money, barter can also help you deal with price controls, currency shortages, excessive taxes, or draconian regulations. In short, barter can help you cut red tape and live much better than you would if you simply relied on currency to carry out all your transactions.

And a word to the wise when you start to practice the techniques outlined in this manual: Use good judgment about who you confide in. Develop a list of trustworthy people, mostly friends and family, to do business with. Be careful, especially about the location of your tangible assets; i.e., where you store your gold and silver. (See "Storing Precious Metals & Valuables" in Appendix E.)

Personal Values - Thrift

Many barterers feel that trading actual commodities also puts their values into good order. Barter reveals what something is worth in terms of the services or goods you have to offer. And that can make you a better shopper and also help you save for what you really <u>need</u> if the "price" of something seems excessive to you. Becoming thrifty is virtuous.

Doing without can be an important strategy in a barter economy. While many of us don't think twice about wasting small sums of money, such spending often nickel-and-dimes us into sore financial straits. This is especially true during an emergency or a situation where the economy is faltering. Then you need to spend wisely, putting the old saw of "use it up, wear it out, do without" into practice.

This also means that in a barter economy, the more self-sufficient you are, the better you can get along. If you're in the position to turn down trades that aren't to your liking, you'll soon discover that people learn to make better initial offers when you're bartering with them. Being able to turn down deals that aren't to your liking will give you an important edge in bargaining.

$100,000 invested in gold and silver coins purchased September,
2015 is now worth $119,000. See our recommended
Model Precious Metals Portfolios (Appendix B).

Be Prepared

It is time to learn to be self-sufficient; during an economic emergency, whether we're talking about a loss of your job or a nation-wide economic collapse, you'll not have much free time to pick up new skills. Learn how to do things yourself; and do some reading. Further, connect with other like-minded people you trust, and develop a network of reliable friends with survival in mind. (Best if your network includes people with complementary talents.) This is very important because if our banks fail (ATM machines don't work) or people don't receive their government or pension checks - violence will be a problem.

Besides having emergency food and water, every family should have some paper money stashed at home in a safe place, but not too much because it loses purchasing power every day. A good rule of thumb is to have at least $1,000 per person in the family, with at least a fourth of it in small bills.

For information about setting up a retreat - out of the city - I recommend you read a new book, Safe House Survival: Step-by-step Beginner's Guide on How to Build, Stockpile and Maintain by Ronald Williams (See details in Appendix F and about many other books and websites in Appendix G.)

If you learn to do some welding, operate specialized equipment, or know how to run a lathe or other wood or metal-working machinery, you'll have skills that can be bartered even if the dollar loses most of its value. Check out some do-it-yourself books from your local library or purchase some "how to" manuals for a special library (also see Appendix F). You'll discover that plumbing, carpentry work, car repair, and similar jobs that you're spending a fortune on aren't all that hard to do yourself, especially the more minor jobs. Now is also the time to stock your shop (even if it's only a corner of your garage). Quality hand tools, nails, screws, and the like will prove valuable during an economic emergency. And such equipment and know-how will also enable you to save some big bills on a day-to-day basis as well.

Another area that can pay off big during economic hard times is a house that has low heating, water, and other utility costs. While it will most likely be impossible to "pull the plug" on your utilities, there are ways to cut back on them through the purchase of low energy appliances, use of wood-burning stoves (even if available just for emergency use), and the like. You should also remember that if things really get dire and the government's money becomes worthless, many utilities will shut down. Then you'll have to be as self-sufficient as you can be.

There are many sources of information on how to survive in a natural or man-made disaster that are not covered in this book, addressing food storage, tools for survival, developing a "bug-out bag," locating sources of water near your home, etc. I'll repeat myself: Purchase some good books on these topics and go to the recommended websites.

Conserving your use of energy and commodities won't guarantee a great standard of living in a barter economy. But wasting what you have can make you poor. Be sure your whole family understands this. Only when everyone pulls together can you save your capital and have surpluses available to barter with others for essentials or even luxury items. If everyone in your family learns to recycle, repair, or substitute for their needs, you'll quickly start to get ahead and be in a much better situation in a barter economy.

For example, the newspapers that you currently lug to the recycling bin might be employed by your family to create a variety of papier-mâché objects, from toys to furniture. All that's needed is some water and some cheap glue (perhaps with an electric blender to help out). Or, the newspaper could be transformed into confetti and mixed with borax instead of glue (to make it flame proof) and used to add insulation to your home. Transform grass clippings and garbage into mulch for a self-sufficient garden (which doesn't need expensive fertilizers).

Be creative and get your family members involved. Some enterprising people use empty pop and milk bottles as the "holes" in concrete that they mix on site, creating a building material that is both insulated and relatively inexpensive, adding onto their homes by using what they'd normally throw away. Outside, it looks like an expensive stucco wall; inside, it's riddled with free building materials normally carried to a landfill. You can do the same types of things if you put your mind to it. (Just because advertisers relentlessly promote buying new things, you don't have to play that game. Stop giving away ''junk'' to be recycled by someone else at a profit and be content with what you have.)

Repairing can also save you a lot of money. Again, we've all been brainwashed into throwing things out and buying completely new items when the originals might easily have been repaired. Often, the right kind of glue or a cheap visit to a repair shop is all that's needed to save a lot of money--or to produce barter materials. Replace things that can't be repaired with something you already have on hand. When in doubt, do without. Chances are that will put you far ahead in the barter game--and ahead in the cash game as well.

Visit RhynesGuide.com to:

- *Setup a FREE 30-minute consultation with Craig Rhyne*
- *Sign up for monthly e-newsletters*
- *Order more books*
- *Access video reports*
- *Live chat: (206) 719-6368*

Types of Barter

MOST PEOPLE THINK that there's just one type of barter. But there are many types and they are often mixed together, creating a wide variety of trading. It's important to be aware of the various types because not knowing how they work can be expensive, just as not knowing how to get the most for your money can be wasteful.

Gift Exchange

The simplest type of barter is an exchange of gifts. In primitive cultures, an exchange of gifts was a trading of physical items. In advanced cultures, the exchange is more often of services or information. Most likely you engage in this type of barter now and don't even realize it. If you're used to saying "I owe you one for this" or you feel compelled to "pay back" someone for a kindness done to you, then you're already operating under the gift barter system whether you realize it or not. People in our culture often *pretend* that gifts are given without the expectation of a return of a like-valued gift. This is rarely the case. Anytime you fail to return a favor or gift, you're risking alienation of the person who gave you the present. This is especially true in a barter economy, though the exchange may just be to "get things started" rather than an end in itself.

Gift exchanges are common between two barterers who engage in trade on a regular basis and want to maintain their friendship. In such case, exchanging gifts establishes rapport. You need to exercise a little finesse in your gift exchange. Trying to hurry things up with this type of trade (as with most forms of barter) is a mistake. So is giving a gift that is obviously less valuable than the one given to you. Failure to obey these unspoken laws will brand you as being rude and may derail any chance of doing bartering with that person in the future.

Two-Trader Deals

Another form of barter is a trade between two individuals who are strangers. This is similar to a gift exchange but permits the traders to haggle about the price or even reject a proposed trade if it doesn't seem fair to each of them. Again, physical objects aren't the only things that can be traded; ideas, information, and services can also be exchanged. It's also possible to trade a number of items on either side of the bargain. Obviously, a person might trade a dozen eggs for a book, for example.

Trades should have comparable value. That means a doctor might barter an office visit while you would have to trade a physical object having the same "cash value" as an office visit before the economy crashed. When services are being traded, the advanced skills of one person will often command more (and less time) on a job than is the case with unskilled work. For example, if you were exchanging yard work for a doctor's visit, the doctor might spend fifteen minutes with you while you spent all day cleaning his yard. For this reason, it's always good to have skills that are "expensive" to trade rather than tasks that anyone can do if they have the time.

Third-Party Barter Arrangements

Another form of barter comes close to being a form of money. It employs the trading of a promised service from one person to a third party uninvolved in the original trade. The doctor in the above example might not need to have any yard work done; in such a case his patient would write, "I promise to do one day's yard work to the bearer of this paper; signed Joe Smith." The doctor could then trade this promissory note to his grocer, who does need some yard work, for a sack of food.

A third-party barter system could easily rival the economy created by a money system, especially if careful records are kept (as can be done with a computer / smart phone). If the world's governments faltered badly during an economic collapse, a third-party barter system might replace banks and many government services, creating a very different culture from what we have now.

Currently there are barter "clubs" that employ some types of credits to exchange or store barter "value" in third-party trades. Members rate each service and determine the number of credits for items and services. Thus, our doctor might get four credits for a fifteen-minute office visit while the yard worker would get only one credit for an hour's work. These credits are then entered into a computer (e.g. spreadsheet) and members of the club exchange their credits for the services of others in the club. These credits become a type of currency, especially as the size of the club expands.

Further, there have been many stories about the creation of crypto-currencies, such as Bitcoin, where non-dollar and non-precious metals credits can be used to purchase items without owners giving their identities. However, there is nothing but speculation backing them, and I do not recommend them at all. Further, I expect the government to clamp down on crypto-currencies and demand unveiling /tracking the transactions in the end. Here's a warning from my friend, Don McAlvany of International Collector's Associates, in his August, 2017 newsletter:

"As an investment, Bitcoin is extremely volatile at best. At worst, the vast majority of investors (98-99% of them) are going to get slaughtered. Your investment could be cut in half (or worse) overnight. Just this summer, one newer cryptocurrency called 'Ethereum' experienced a "flash crash" when it fell by 96%. It fell from $315 to $13 in a matter of seconds. The currency quickly rebounded, but not before some traders were completely wiped out.

"So if you're looking to invest in currencies, Bitcoin and other crypto-currencies are too volatile and are trading much too high to even consider at this point. Their volatility, coupled with network reliability problems, coming government regulation, and security issues, makes these mathematical holograms the riskiest currency speculations of our generation. And it will not remain private from government scrutiny (spying)."

Because of the cash-like effect of barter and crypto-currency credits, the IRS has come down hard on such clubs making them less than attractive for most people in the US as long as the currency remains relatively stable. But you can bet that such clubs will spring up during a black market. If you decide to join such a club, you should be cautious, however, since the computerized records will lead back to each member if the government decides to outlaw such transactions or tax them out of existence.

Middleman Barter

Another type of barter is the "middleman" trade. In this type of barter an individual acts as the middleman and has nothing tangible to trade; he only locates two people with items to trade. The middleman then makes each of the two people aware of the tradeable goods and introduces them to each other, facilitating the barter exchange. In such a case, the middleman earns a commission as a gift from both of the parties involved in the actual trade. As with other "gifts" in barter, it is important that each party gives a sufficient gift to the middleman for his efforts. Otherwise, they won't be brought into any more of the trades he arranges.

If the economy has completely broken down and the government is intent on preventing barter, or if the lawlessness of an area makes it hard to barter without the danger of being robbed, another type of middleman might spring up. In this case the middleman would provide a safe place to conduct trades. This middleman would act as a policeman, most likely be armed and capable of throwing out or otherwise dealing with any unruly person or someone intent on robbing others. If society and safety is seriously compromised, such middlemen may have to pay the local law officials and politicians to keep the barter area in operation.

Bribery and policing to create a black marketing area are expensive endeavors. In such a situation, things could become dangerous in a hurry with a change in government or government policy. But such a middleman supervised barter area would be safer than trying to conduct trading in the open. Again, those interested in trading would pay the middleman with gifts. Unsuitable gifts wouldn't open the door to the bartering area but generous gifts would.

Due to the danger of this last form of barter, it's probably best to avoid such places. The safest type of barter is between two people with no one else involved. Such trades can generally be conducted at a person's home or their business during times when there are few customers that could overhear what's going on. This is especially true if both of the traders are friends and meet together from time to time anyway. In such a situation it would be rare to run into problems. And dealing with trusted friends and family keeps you away from government attempts to tax or stamp out an underground economy.

"Horse Traders"

The final type of barter involves a type of person that is known in barter circles as a "horse trader." Unlike most barterers who are happy to exchange something for another object or service of like value, horse traders attempt to make extra profits on their deals. Consequently, they're very skilled at barter and some may be on the shady side, often exaggerating the value of what they have or, in extreme cases, misrepresenting items entirely.

Horse traders often have to travel because people soon stop trading with them if they feel they've been swindled in a trade. You should always be on the lookout for a stranger who has a trade that looks too good to be true. Avoid the temptation to become a horse trader since trust is key to successful bartering and you want to be known as trustworthy.

Barter is based on the idea of fair exchange. Just as in any economy, when everyone feels like they are getting a fair value for what they're trading, they aren't apt to grumble about things. When they feel they've been taken advantage of, they won't want to bargain with such a person again. Aim to be fair and you'll have plenty of people with whom to trade.

Gold and Silver as Money

In the event the dollar loses significant purchasing power - such as through hyperinflation - gold and silver coins and bars will be ideal for trading with others to get the items you want. (See "Best Coins for Barter," Appendix A.)

Arguably, gold and silver coins are "real money," so exchanges of ounces of precious metals for goods and services are not acts of "barter" in the classic sense. However, until society returns to thinking of gold and silver coins as "money," rather than investment coins (or just "commodities"), we must consider how to "barter" one's coins and bars to acquire what we need in a distressed economy where the paper money is failing.

The economy need not be in utter turmoil to barter with gold and silver, however. When my oldest son was born in 1978, I paid the doctor his fee at a "birth clinic" with four British Sovereign gold coins (see the story below).

$25,000 in gold and silver coins purchased 9/10/2015;
Now worth $29,700 (September, 2017). See Model
Precious Metals Portfolios, Appendix B.

Barter Tactics

Many people think that barter means "free;" that they can trade their "junk" for things they need and, seemingly, get the new goods for free. It's a big mistake to think of things being bartered this way. Anything you can trade for something you need has value. It may not have value to you, but it nevertheless has value. For the same reason, you should remember that you'll never have an unlimited amount of "stuff" to barter. Just as you can run out of money, so, too, you can run out of barter capital. Once you've bartered all you have, you won't be able to trade any more.

Of course, there's one big plus with barter; you can trade off tangible items you've previously received. But there's a catch in that people's needs and wants change. What you once wanted, but now want to barter, may not be something someone wants now. This puts you at a disadvantage. The secret is never barter all you have to trade, just as you wouldn't spend everything in your checking account or run up charges on credit cards up to their credit limits.

Best Foot Forward - Making Things Happen

When you're bartering, you need to put on your "salesman hat." Just don't become too much like the used-car-salesman cliché. Put your best foot forward and try to drum up trades if things are slow. Propose a barter trade with a friend or neighbor and you'll often get one; sit around waiting for a deal to come along and nothing will happen.

The larger the barter deal, the greater the need to "break the ice" with a small gift to start things on an even footing. If, for example, you were creating jewelry to barter, you might make a small tie tack. Then, give one to the person you're trading with: "So, you can see what my handiwork looks like these days."

Time

When bartering, it's important to use your time wisely. Make small trades quickly; spend more time dickering over the "price" with larger trades. It's important not to rush trades involving a lot of materials or items of great value. If you get into a hurry, the person you're bartering may think you're trying to pull a fast one or that you are trying to complete the deal before he has time to realize what's going on. Take your time so a deal won't go sour on you. Very large contracts may entail negotiations over the course of several days.

Large trades with strangers can also be facilitated more comfortably if one or both of those involved provides "references" of people you've previously traded with. This doesn't have to be formal. If you can just drop the name of a few well-known and trusted people this may be all that's needed.

Buyer Beware

Always be cautious when trading for anything that might be dangerous if it malfunctions or if it is not what it appears to be. Medication, machinery, heating equipment, and the like should come from sources you trust. Discovering that the penicillin you bartered for is terribly outdated or bogus could prove a fatal mistake. Likewise, a defective heater that was too good a deal to pass up might burn your home down. When you're bartering, especially if you're in black market conditions, you must take great care to avoid being cheated and endangered.

Remember that the government has little vested interest in preventing fraud among those operating outside financial transactions overseen by the government. For this reason don't expect to be protected from shady dealers or horse traders. This will be especially the case if you're bartering in black-market conditions.

Seasonal Demand

Demand for various commodities changes over time and, with many goods, is seasonal. This means you can get the best deal on a coat, for example, if you barter for one in the middle of the summer when demand for coats is low. Likewise, if you have a coat to trade, storing it until the beginning of winter would be a good ploy. The same is true of garden produce and many other goods.

If you can learn to store, process, can, or otherwise preserve seasonal goods, you'll be able to trade items when they are in high demand, rather than when demand is low. For the same reason, you should look for barter deals where the person trading with you has a product "out of season." This places what he's trading "on sale" so you can get more in the trade. When possible, you should trade with people who have plenty. Such people enter into barter arrangements with a take-it-or-leave-it attitude that, at first, might appear to be to your disadvantage. This state of mind puts less pressure on both sides of the barter exchange. Often, the people who are the most pushy when bartering or who will try to jerk your chain are people who don't have much to trade. Worse yet are those who have become desperate. If you want to engage in charity, that should be your choice; don't position yourself in a trade that pressures you to do so against your will.

The First Trade

The first time you engage in a barter deal with someone, it's a good idea to give them the best part of the deal. This makes the person feel good and lays the ground work for the next trade you will make with them. More than likely it will also help establish your reputation for giving good deals. Such a reputation will help bring more trades in the future.

It's also important to make trading with you a pleasant experience. As with any business, your goal should be to have satisfied customers.

Don't try high pressure tactics or seem too clever. Do make every effort to remain pleasant and friendly, even when you run into "horse traders" who try high-pressure tactics. A good name is impossible to buy and will bring people to you when they have something they think you'd be interested in trading.

Getting Good Deals

Being polite doesn't mean you can't get good bargains in your trades. One way to lever exchanges in your favor is to make it appear that the item the other person is offering is not all that useful to you. Savvy barterers always have a reason why they really don't need something all that much--but will trade for it anyway if the "price" is right.

Another way to argue for a lower price is to point out apparent faults in what is being offered for trade. For example, if someone is offering a green coat, you might employ the tack that you'd prefer a blue one. Or that you aren't that fond of the double-breasted style. Or that it seems a little light for a winter coat. This can be done diplomatically and, provided you stick to just one or two faults, you can generally point out faults without stepping on the other trader's toes.

Oddly enough, it's better not to point out obvious flaws. The reason for this is that the person offering an item for barter will be aware of its most obvious flaws and will have already discounted it because of the flaws. Both to assure yourself that you're getting something that's in good shape as well as to determine if there are any perceived faults, always carefully inspect anything offered to you. This will ensure that the deal is good. (If the person offering an object starts to get surly when you inspect something or tries to distract your attention, chances are high that something's wrong so you should be extra cautious about the deal.) If you discover anything odd or have doubts about an object, ask a few questions to find out more about it. People who are anxious for a trade will usually volunteer information and may even point out faults that you'd missed in your inspection. If you can't think of anything else, ask the person why he wants to trade the object.

Bad Tactics

Sometimes a pair of traders will work together, adopting "good cop, bad cop" tactics. In such a case, one member of the duo will keep finding fault or suggest that the team is getting the bad end of the deal. The other member will smooth things over and appear to be trying to help out the person the pair is bartering with. This tactic will eventually be discovered and is most popular with horse traders. You're better off not doing this and avoiding those who do.

If you're bartering something that is broken or doesn't operate properly, you should make it clear that the item is being traded "as is." This means that it most likely needs some repair work or is perhaps only useful for parts. You should also keep this in mind when trading for something that is offered "as is." "As is" goods can sometimes be repaired and traded for a better deal. If you're able to repair machinery, computers, or whatever, finding goods that are being offered "as is" might be a real bonus for you. Of course, if you can't repair something, then you will most likely be better off avoiding it.

Additional Tricks

With very large objects, livestock, or other heavy or awkward materials, part of the deal that you can throw into your bargain is moving the item to the new owner's property. Often this will swing a deal because many people interested in owning such things may not have a way to transport them. The inability to transport things presents people with an extra hassle that often is enough to make them reject a deal. If you offer to deliver it, they may trade for it.

It's always best to let the person bringing something to you to set their "price" on what they have to trade. Often, by letting them do this, you'll obtain something for less than you would have bartered for it if you'd made the offer up front. The biggest trick in such a case is hiding your surprise at his offer. If the price is too high, just make a counter offer.

If a seasoned trader won't make a first offer, then it's up to you to launch the initial offer. In such case, it's wise to ask for a better deal than you expect to actually trade for, this gives you a little maneuvering room. You don't want to make an outlandishly low offer, however, since the trader will decide you want too much and that he'll be wasting his time if he continues to dicker on the price with you.

"Dickering" is haggling over the final trade. It consists of offers and counter-offers, as well as the inspection of what's being traded for flaws and the introduction of reasons why the object isn't as valuable to you as the price being asked. This can get very complicated and will continue until both parties are pleased with the final offer or one or the other doesn't think the trade will be to his benefit and quits.

"To Boot"

When the negotiations near an end, often the final bargain is struck when one or the other of the traders adds something "to boot." For example, if two people were haggling over the trade of two vehicles, one might argue that theirs is worth more. The other trader, if he's intent on making a deal, might offer a spare set of tires "to boot" in addition to the vehicle itself. Often the numbers and types of materials added "to boot" can become quite detailed and may complicate the main trade. Things offered "to boot" can come from either side of the bargain. One trader might, for example, ask for a pair of tires "to boot" or the other trader might offer to change the oil.

It's always wise to have items of varying values ready to offer to complete a trade. Hide them from view if possible, holding them in reserve to complete the deal. By having a range of such items, you can employ the one that is least expensive but will still probably end in a deal. If you know you'll be trading with a friend and have a good idea about what his likes and dislikes are, and what he needs, you can often select a small "to boot" item that will be perfect for the final negotiation.

Take Your Time

Stalling is a tactic most seasoned barterers employ. Being in a hurry is usually a weakness in a barter exchange, and this will often cause a deal to fail or force the person in a hurry to lose out (or cause them to prematurely lower their price). During this period, offers and counter-offers are made, both sides examine the objects being traded, and major faults are pointed out in an attempt to get the price lowered. If one side of the barter is hesitant, then the other will throw material or services "to boot" into the mix and things either go forward or the trade will fail. One or both parties may ask for time to think over the exchange; in such a case, care must be taken to limit the time or specify that if a better offer comes along, it will be taken.

Some traders become very adept at conducting a war of nerves during extended negotiations. Some of their tactics include: Making outrageously low offers for something, acting confused about the offer ("Let me get this straight…"), or causing distractions. Occasionally, you'll run into people who want to barter simply to waste time. These people won't finalize a trade unless you're giving things away. If this appears to be the case, then you should adopt a take-it-or-leave-it policy and end the exercise.

Scarcity and Tales of Woe

Because objects gain more value if they are scarce, displaying only one of whatever you have to trade rather than the whole lot can give greater apparent value to what you're trading. For example, if you had five 1/10 oz gold coins and were prepared to trade only two, you should display only two. This makes them appear more scarce and creates the psychological effect of the coins having a greater value than if they were all displayed at the same time. Exploit this apparent scarcity of products in the barter negotiations. "I don't know, these are my last coins. Do you want them or not?"

When traders are desperate to get something in barter, they may adopt a tale of woe to gain sympathy for their trade. If you want to help people, that's fine. But you shouldn't do so by making poor deals when you're bartering. If you do, word will soon spread and people will expect you to cut them favors, too, and they will be resentful if you don't.

Price Gouging

You must avoid lowering your price beyond a certain point. Unfortunately, after a certain stage, a person starts to think that an object will be given away because the price keeps being lowered on it. When an unreasonably low proposal is made to you, counter with a higher price and then lower it slightly as the dickering continues. If you lower it excessively, you'll discover that the person you're trading with will start thinking even that price is too high. He'll want it lowered--perhaps below his original offer. You're better off to stop dickering rather than lowering your ask price too much.

"Damaged" Goods

Another ploy used by traders is to have "damaged goods" or "seconds" available in reserve when a potential deal is about to fail because the "price" isn't quite right. For example, if you were offering a hunting rifle and the person looking it over thought it was just a tad too nice (and expensive) for the pile of silver dollars he had, and if he had nothing to boot, you could substitute a less expensive rifle (provided you had one). This permits lowering your price without appearing to do so.

Finalizing the Exchange

Sometimes, when a deal is very close to being finalized but the person you're bargaining with can't seem to come to a decision, you can give signals that you're ready to quit and that you're going to look elsewhere for a trade. Often when a person sees a deal about to fail, and considers the time spent in dickering as well as the fact that he'd like to have what you're offering, he'll decide to go ahead and make the trade. If he doesn't, you've probably saved yourself some time.

Once a deal is completed, the actual exchange of goods, services, or whatever should take place as soon as possible. This prevents a host of problems, including the breakage of what has been traded (and who pays for its repair), substitution of items, changes in the value of goods due to swings in the market8i, as well as unforseen developments that affect the parties or the merchandise.

You should never change your price after settling on a trade agreement. Dicker all you want before a trade; but once the agreement is finalized, you must live withthe deal. This unspoken tradition of barter can lead to problems if you settle on a "price" but one party wants to think it over. In such a case, you should set a deadline after which the trade is no longer a "done deal." Failure to do this can cause mix-ups and misunderstandings. Since barter is based on trust, this is the last thing you want to happen.

With very complex trades, especially if some time passes while someone is thinking about things or before the objects will actually be exchanged, it's wise to write down the exact terms of the agreement, perhaps even having both parties involved signing the document. Such a "contract" won't likely have the power of a real contract (though it might, so be careful what you sign), especially if you're operating in a black market. But the paper will help everyone remember the terms, which can be hard to do after an extended time of offers and counter offers. If one party remembers the terms to be what were really his counter offer and not the deal itself, the paper may help jog his memory.

Further, especially in complicated barter exchanges, it can be quite good to have a witness who, if needed, can later attest to the details of the agreement made.

Getting Ready to Barter

The time to get ready for bartering is before you have to do it. Now is the time to convert at least 10% (up to 25%) of your assets into gold, silver, and platinum coins. Now is the time to take an inventory of the items or skills you have that might be bartered. Now is the time to practice your bartering abilities, and have some fun. And now is the time to start discussing these things with people you trust, thus developing a network of folks who may come to be of great importance to you in the future.

Practicing

Good places to practice bartering include flea markets, gunshops, and anywhere commodities are traded freely. Many large cities have "swap meets" where everyone brings whatever they want to trade for something else. Secondhand shops, antique stores, or other businesses that allow you to haggle over the prices of things being sold can provide the venues where you can develop the skills you need to get good at bartering.

Plan Ahead

DURING TIMES OF crisis, some objects become more valuable because they are hard to obtain. Good old supply versus demand. If you think about what might become scarce in your area, and then stock up on it while it's cheap, you can create a barter storehouse that will tide you over during a period when barter becomes the name of the game.

Traditionally, the items that are the most valuable in barter economies are water, food, sufficient clothing, transportation, gold and silver coins, medical necessities, and some luxury items. "Junk silver" pre-1965 silver coins (eg, dimes and quarters), gold coins (especially 1/10 and 1/4 oz sizes), and possibly some gems / jewelry will allow you to trade for most anything. One of the best attributes of gold and silver coins is that they are a convenient, concentration of value. And, if you had to leave your home quickly - violent desperate people at your door - it would be quite an advantage if you had gold and silver coins in your "bug out bag." (See "Best Coins for Barter," Appendix A, and "Storing Precious Metals & Valuables," Appendix E.)

American Eagle Gold and Silver Coins

Necessities can be stored, provided you have the storage space for them and provided they have a long shelf life. For example, if you live in an apartment with scant space, then you might store a wealth of small necessities like needles, ammunition, or medicines. But you couldn't corner the market on unprocessed wheat or copper wiring--you wouldn't have the room.

Likewise, while bread might become scarce during an emergency, you can't simply run out and buy a truckload, store it somewhere, and expect to have anything worth trading four years from now (unless there's a big market for bread mold). However, you could store sealed drums of wheat that could be employed as a basic component for making bread. (Wheat in sealed drums filled with an inert gas lasts almost forever if kept cool and dry.) Note: You should have at least a 3-month supply of food and water, which is why you should go to the Legacy Food Storage website and consider various options: **www.legacyfoodstorage.com. Enter code "WGE" at checkout to receive a 10% discount on all items.**

Organize a storage area with floor to ceiling shelves, and stock up on glass jars, lids, canning supplies (including a plastic funnel for filling jars), and a micrometer that would be useful to check the dimensions of coins, two precise scales (one for weighing coins; at least one that does not use batteries), tape measures, measuring cups and large containers.

Other possible items you might consider stockpiling for trade during a crisis include large amounts of salt, pepper, soaps, detergents, granola / energy bars by the case, vitamins and mineral supplements, cigarettes, various fifths of hard liquor, paper towels, matches, canned milk, powdered milk, soups, toilet paper, 5-gallon containers of water, gasoline, grain mills, water filter units, vinegar, and sugar. The list goes on and on. Tools can also be of great value. However, given the large number of do-it-yourself tools currently gathering dust in home shops, you might expect to initially see many of these traded off for very little during an emergency.

Unlike tools, the fasteners and accessories they use might be in short supply. A barrel of nails, screws, or staples might be very valuable, for example. As might glue gun sticks or glue itself (although most glue has a finite shelf-life making it a little iffy for long-term storage). The exception to the low-value-tool rule will be specialized tools that you can use. If you're planning on bartering a skill, then you need to stock any tools that might break and any supplies you might run low on. If you need electricity to power tools (and hand tools can't be substituted), you might even consider purchasing an electrical generator and a good quantity of fuel for it. (Use special, protected containers and fuel additives that help maintain the octane level.) This would enable you to continue working during a power outage or if the utilities are forced to close. If you make plans beforehand, you can practically corner the market and offer specialized services that are quite valuable.

Firearms have traditionally been something everyone perceives as being needed during an emergency. However, the U.S. is awash in guns; that means during an emergency there may be many firearms up for trade. What is less likely to be available, and easier for you to obtain now, is ammunition. Most gun owners have only a box or two of ammunition for any firearm they own. If you have some ammunition to trade, you'll have something they want and will pay dearly for. Stock up and have a minimum of 500 to 1,000 rounds for each of your guns. Even better is to acquire double or triple these amounts to have ammunition to barter with.

If you're living in a rural area (or an area where the law permits), you should raise small animals and grow a garden that will give you meat and produce. You might raise chickens for their eggs, have a goat(s) for milk, and plant rows of berries and a garden for fresh vegetables; all would provide valuable barter commodities during an emergency and would feed your family whether there's an emergency or not. As with other skills, raising livestock and food isn't something you learn overnight. If you're intent on doing this, you need to start learning now, before the pressure is on for you to produce.

Although knowledge isn't always power, having reference books, how-to manuals, and other resources can also be a great asset any time and especially during an emergency. A book on plumbing or electrical wiring might, for example, enable you to make repairs on your home when plumbers and electricians are unavailable or too expensive. Such a book might even give you a new skill to barter. (See recommended books and websites, Appendix F and Appendix G.)

Defense

Because a barter economy often goes hand-in-hand with reduced law enforcement services, possibly even anarchy, you should also be able to defend yourself, your family, and your supplies. Being skilled at bartering will do little good if the first thug who crosses your path steals you blind. Traditionally, the tool that's suited for self-defense has been a pistol or other firearm. Of course, it's outside the scope of this manual to cover the best guns for such a purpose; and whether you want to carry and perhaps use a firearm to defend yourself is a choice you'll need to make for yourself. You should, at least, give some thought to what you'll do if confronted by a lawless individual intent on robbing you. Familiarize yourself with gunshops in your area and do business with them. And be sure that you (and your family members) know how to use their weapons; take firearm safety classes.

Ruger 9 MM Pistol

Being armed will reduce the likelihood that you'll be robbed. So will presenting yourself modestly. Drive a low-cost, older model of car. Don't wear flashy clothing, and don't make a habit of wearing large gold rings or the like. In this way, you will avoid being seen as a potential target by a robber. Even if your bartering skills make you rich, you shouldn't flaunt your wealth. Low-profile living is the best way to avoid attracting unwanted attention.

Valuable Barter Skills

Even if you only develop barter skills as a hobby, you'll have an important talent that could make a big difference in your family's ability to survive during an extended economic emergency or in the event of a natural disaster. And that could be a very important plus. Further, should we be able to avoid a financial emergency, barter skills will help you in your negotiations the rest of your life.

Other Important Preparations

Besides learning how to barter and making provisions for your safety and finances, you need to be ready for natural and manmade disasters that affect your health. Everyone should have a robust First-Aid kit at home and a smaller version in your car(s). Further, keep extra bandages, scissors, painkillers and back-up prescription medicines. (See Appendix D, page 99)

Recommended Money Managers

If you have an investment portfolio of $500,000 or more, you may want to work with a wealth management or financial advisory company. I have chosen three (out of hundreds) because I know these individuals and they understand how vulnerable our economy is. And they do not pooh-pooh the importance of owning physical precious metals to diversify one's portfolio.

Larry Knudsen, Hightower Advisors Bellevue,
WA office. (425) 455-6623
Email: lknudsen@hightoweradvisors.com

Ed McCahill, Ronald Blue Trust, Bothell, WA office.
(425) 485-0380. Email: ed.mccahill@ronblue.com.
With nationwide trust capabilities, Ronald Blue Trust provides
wealth management strategies and trust services based on Biblical

principles to help clients make wise financial decisions, live generously, and leave a lasting legacy.

<u>Byron Piro</u>, Piro Levon Washington Wealth Management Group of Wells Fargo Advisors, Bellevue, WA. (425) 646-4860
Email: byron.piro@wfadvisors.com

<u>Greg Zanetti</u>, Zanetti Financial (clearing through Charles Schwab), Albuquerque, NM (505) 250-3754
Email: gjzanetti@live.com

Visit <u>RhynesGuide.com</u> to:

- *Setup a FREE 30-minute consultation with Craig Rhyne*
- *Sign up for monthly e-newsletters*
- *Order more books*
- *Access video reports*
- *Live chat: (206) 719-6368*

Why and How to Barter
with Gold and Silver

THE U.S. FEDERAL debt is now more than $20 TRILLION, <u>not</u> counting unfunded liabilities such as Social Security, Medicare and Medicaid. Meanwhile, foreigners have increasingly noticed that the U.S. Dollar is losing purchasing power and we expect a major "re-set" of our financial system to occur with great pain. Those who own old U.S. pre-1965 90% silver dimes, quarters, half-dollars and old silver dollars, various sizes of silver rounds and bars, and gold (and platinum) coins and bars will be able to trade for food, water, transportation, etc. There will be, in the words of a deceased friend Dr. Hans Sennholz, an "acceleration of information," where the average citizen will very quickly learn what's happening.

The International Monetary Fund (IMF) has stated the global "Money Standard Shift" will be concluded after the next big financial crisis. This dollar "re-set" will forever change the reserve currency status of the U.S. Dollar, overturning the Bretton Woods agreement put in place in 1945 as the "reserve currency" of the world. The "almighty dollar" will be replaced by a basket of currencies reflecting these financial realities: 1) Foreigners are purchasing less and less of our debt / bonds because they recognize our debt levels are insurmountable; 2) the BRICS nations (Brazil, Russia, India, China and South Africa) are now making trade agreements in their respective currencies between themselves, not in terms of U.S. dollars; 3) The gold formerly held by the U.S. and by Americans has been moving systematically from the west to the east, especially to China and Russia. And, as the Golden Rule states: "He who owns the gold makes the rules."

We do not know the timing of the financial "reset" - when the International Monetary Fund (IMF) will act in concert with the Federal Reserve and the world's central banks. However, it will probably be quick and utterly shocking. Unless there is a return to the "gold standard," there will be bank closures, ATMs will fail, the government will establish very restrictive "capital controls," and precious metals will sky-rocket. The government will declare an emergency and after some months, there will be violence in the streets. We could wake up tomorrow, or in three months, or a year from now, with gold up $500 or more overnight. In such case, the exchanges (and most dealers) would only have "bids," no "ask offers." Dealers such as my company Washington Gold Exchange would be open to buy or sell gold, silver, platinum, etc., but we would be constricted because of limited supplies. For this reason, you are wise to acquire coins now while they are readily available and deliveries are relatively quick.

The simple answer to why gold and silver will be the best items to barter with is that they are "real money," and they have 6,000 years of history in their favor. One of the best reasons they are the premier barter item is that they are very transportable (gold more than silver). And, it is rare to find a person who will always have the "right" item to barter. There will be many cases where the person you are dealing with has enough of the items that you offer. But they will exchange the items you want for silver or gold coins because they know they can be used to trade for something else they want in the future.

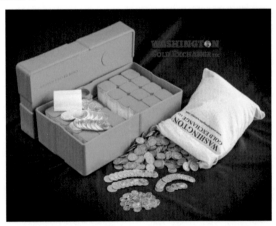

$50,000 in gold and silver coins purchased 9/10/2015;
Now worth $59,400 (September, 2017).
See Model Precious Metals Portfolios, Appendix B.

Recommendation:
Best Coins for Barter

SINCE FOUNDING C. Rhyne & Associates in 1974, I have recommended purchasing silver - in the form of Pre-1965 90% silver dimes, quarters and halves - as the first step when you buy precious metals. These small coins provide you small denominations for bartering for everyday goods and services. (See Appendix A, with our recommendations for silver and gold coins. Then go to Appendix B, "Model Precious Metals Portfolios," for the number of coins you would get based on various budgets.) If possible, own at least one full "bag" of old, circulated 90% silver coins, defined as $1,000 face. (A full bag weighs about 55 lbs., but we deliver them in two half-bags.) After these, you should get 1 ounce silver coins: either American Eagles, Canadian Maple Leafs, Austrian Philharmonics, Australian Kangaroo coins, or 1 ounce silver rounds, such as Sunshine Mint, Buffaloes, or any number of other brands of small bars or rounds that have their weight in silver stamped on them.

Once you have silver, buy gold (and possibly platinum) coins. Depending on your finances, keep liquidity and tradability in mind and contemplate how easy (or difficult) it would be to barter with someone if your coins were "too valuable." What I mean is that you would want small coins, such as silver dimes, to trade for a loaf of bread. You might use 1/10 and 1/4 ounce gold coins for bartering for items such as a large battery or for tires. If you have substantial funds, you should have some of the 1/2 and 1 ounces coins, especially since they have smaller premiums over their gold content (economies of scale). However, I think it's worth it to pay the premiums for the little coins because of their excellent tradability. As I tell clients: "When gold is $5,000 per ounce, or $10,000 per ounce, it will be awfully nice to have 1/10 ounce coins that are worth, roughly, $500 or $1,000, respectively. When gold goes that high, a one ounce coin would be worth $5,000 or $10,000, and who would be able to handle such a transaction?"

Careful thought has been put into the selection of coins for the Model Precious Metals Portfolios (Appendix B) <u>with barter in mind</u>. Note that we recommend a bigger percentage of silver in the smaller portfolios than in the larger ones. This has been done because the first step in preparation is to have "lower value" silver coins (as compared to gold) for small transactions. Then, because storage space requirements are more daunting for silver, i.e., gold takes so much less room, we have a bigger percentage of gold (and add platinum) in the larger portfolios, $25,000 up to $250,000.

$500,000 in gold, silver and platinum coins purchased 9/10/2015, Now worth $595,000 two years later. Yellow and green "monster boxes" contain 1 ounce Silver Maple Leafs and American Eagles. (See Model Precious Metals Portfolios in Appendix B.)

There are hundreds of coins that have been minted over the ages, from all over the world. Except for "gold bullion coins" that were first created by South Africa with the Krugerrand (in 1967), most all other coins have "odd weights." For example, the wonderful British Sovereign has a gold content of .2354 Troy oz, and the gold content is not stamped on the coin. Because assessing the value of the non-standard sizes of older coins, I recommend that - after you first acquire silver coins - get a good supply of "modern gold bullion coins."

Step 1: <u>Old, pre-1965 Silver Coins</u>. The "first step" in owning precious metals is acquiring pre-1965 U.S. 90% silver dimes, quarters, halves, and dollars. Even though these old dimes, quarters and halves have "odd weights" and the silver content is not imprinted on the coins, they are recognizable and trusted. (And most people know the old silver coins have real silver, and this understanding will become ubiquitous.)

Pre-1965 90% silver coins come in 1/10, 1/4, 1/2 and full $1,000 face bags. Pictured above are uncirculated coins, yet "junk bags" have a lower premium and are comprised of circulated coins. Denominations are not mixed and are delivered in heavy canvas bags. See Model Precious Metals Portfolios in Appendix B.

My second recommendation for silver barter coins is to get the American Silver Eagles, the Australian 1 oz Silver Kangaroos (or other Australian animals), the Austrian 1 oz Silver Philharmonics, and the Canadian Silver Maples Leafs. Why? Because these coins are issued by sovereign governments, they are exactly one ounce of pure silver, and the person bartering with you will probably know of them. Having a mix of them is good - since one person may have heard of Silver Maple Leafs and not any of the others. Additionally, there are many silver "rounds" minted by private mints, in many sizes, including 1/10 oz, 1/4 oz, 1/2 oz and 1 full ounce that offer even more portfolio diversification (and the 1 oz "rounds" sell for about $1 per ounce less than the sovereign government coins).

Check out pictures of recommended silver and gold coins, along with detailed specifications and price indications, in Appendix A. Then consider our various "Model Portfolios" in Appendix B with our recommendation of the proper mix / allocations based on investment amounts of $2,500 to $500,000 (see pages 93 and 94).

Step 2: <u>Small gold coins</u>. After you take Step 1 and have some small <u>silver</u> coins for barter, then get some small gold coins. Since we live in America, it is logical to acquire the American Gold Eagles <u>first</u>, in 1/10 and 1/4 oz sizes. Then, as shown in Appendix A, we list our second highest recommended gold bullion coins (in 5 sizes, including 1/20 oz), the Canadian Gold Maple Leafs. We like these coins because we are a key trading partner with Canada, we are in close proximity to Canada, and because of the fact that they have no alloy (for strength, as with the American Eagles). The Canadian gold coins are .9999 fine gold (24K pure), and this is very appealing to most Asian-Americans. So once you have enough American Eagle gold coins, acquire some Canadian coins. Further, if your funds allow, diversify further with the fractional ounce coins from Australia, Austria, Great Britain, China, South Africa, and possibly with old, circulated U.S. $5 gold pieces (not fancy grades).

Step 3: <u>1/2 ounce and 1 oz gold coins</u>. When you have at least five ounces total in small gold coins (complementing your silver coins), purchase 1/2 and 1 oz coins per Appendix A and Appendix B. In Appendix A, I have included photos of various sizes of the American Eagles, the old U.S. $5, $10, and $20 gold pieces, the American Buffalo, the Canadian Maple Leafs, the

Australian Kangaroo, the Austrian Philharmonic, and the British Britannia. We have provided a list of other gold coins - a second tier - because they meet the important criteria of coming in exact gold weights (1/10, 1/4, 1/2 and 1 oz; also various coins in gram units) and their weights are indicated on the coins. In a barter situation, these aspects of the coins would be very important. However, keep in mind that the best known coins are the American Eagles and Canadian Maple Leafs, and when bartering, this is an advantage. See the chart in Appendix A listing these other fine coin options. Note that there are approximately 50 million South African Krugerrands that freely trade around the world, and they come in the "standard sizes:" 1/10, 1/4, 1/2 and 1 oz. Arguably, holding Krugerrands may be just as good as owning American Eagles or Canadian Maple Leafs.

Step 4: Old U.S. $10 and $20 gold pieces (pre-1933). Besides the old $5 Liberty gold pieces, I recommend the old, circulated $10 and $20 gold pieces. However, notice that I recommend the Very Fine (VF) up to Almost Uncirculated (AU) conditions, not the fancy grades that are often certified and mounted in hard plastic holders. (See Coin Grading / Condition and Glossary of Terms, Appendix I and Appendix J.) The old U.S. gold coins are a stunning part of our history and they are considered "numismatic coins" - thus probably exempt from any future government attempts to have Americans turn in their gold.

Also, in order to make the coins last longer (because they were circulated as money), most governments made their gold coins by alloying the gold with copper, which is why the old U.S. gold pieces, the modern American Eagles and many other coins (see Best Coins for Barter, Appendix A) are 21.6K (900 fine). The amount of pure gold for the modern issues (not counting the copper) is part of their names, e.g., "1 oz Gold American Eagle." However, for the old U.S. gold pieces, the "Fine Gold Content" is listed separately in Appendix, page 112.

Note: I do not cover the complicated topic of numismatic (rare) coins in this book. The numismatic field is well established and provides many exciting hours of fascinating enjoyment for collectors. However, since a focus of this book is barter, I recommend only purchasing "semi-numismatic" gold and silver coins. By this, I mean circulated / common date but old silver dollars and the $5, $10 and $20 gold pieces (Liberty Head and St. Gaudens).

The liquidity / tradability of exceptionally rare coins and <u>high-grade</u> old coins is reduced because only a relatively small subset of investors have such an interest. Some of these coins are so rare that their owners have to take them to auction houses to liquidate them. Further, when markets become extremely volatile, dealers have less time to equivocate about rare dates and mint marks. In such cases, people not knowledgeable about numismatics would not want to pay the high premiums for them over "bullion coins" which basically trade for the intrinsic value of the gold or silver in the coins. Generally speaking, this means that unless there are some real bargains, I do not promote the certified, "slabbed" Mint State (MS) coins. However, owning some truly numismatic coins is appropriate in some cases. (See Appendix I to learn about coin grades / conditions and Appendix J for a Glossary of Terms.)

Old $20 Liberty Head gold pieces in Almost Uncirculated (AU) condition.

Step 5: <u>Platinum coins.</u> Platinum is far more rare than gold, and it is not ubiquitously found like gold. It comes, primarily, from South Africa and Russia, with some smaller production mines in Canada and Montana. For centuries, platinum has traded at about 20% higher than gold, but as of the publication of this book, it is selling at a 24% discount to gold. Since most people know that platinum is superior to gold, e.g. the platinum credit card versus the gold credit card, and there is more industrial demand for platinum than for gold, I see a "platinum play" that will propel the price of platinum to its traditional premium over gold.

When the financial "re-set" occurs, there will be a mad scramble to "quality," read "tangible assets." In such case, Americans will try to buy gold, silver, platinum, diamonds, rubies, sapphires, etc. with trillions of paper dollars that are losing purchasing power quickly. Note, however, that the tradability of the more exotic items, such as platinum, palladium, rare earth minerals, or diamonds, etc. is less than that of small silver and gold coins. So I don't recommend you put any funds into platinum unless you are investing $100,000 or more. Then, no more than 10%. (See Model Precious Metals Portfolios, Appendix B.)

With my caveat stated above, it is worth noting that the first time gold went above $1,000 (in 2007), platinum went briefly to $2,500. This demonstrates the fact that owning platinum can be quite good, with "profit potential" because of its scarcity and industrial demand. Similarly, palladium has industrial demand and has moved up nearly as high as platinum - $946 on 9/1/2017.

Fortunately, there are many good options for buying platinum and palladium, including many private mint bars (such as PAMP) and platinum versions of the American Eagle, Australian Koalas and Platypus coins, Austrian Philharmonics, and the venerable Canadian Maple Leafs. They come in the standard sizes, 1/10, 1/4, 1/2 and 1 oz, yet not all sizes in all years. (Strangely, the Australians have also minted 2 and 10 oz versions of the Koala coins, as well as a kilogram coin.) Additionally, we like the Platinum Noble coins from the Isle of Man, which were the first platinum bullion coins ever issued, between 1983 and 1989. Besides many sizes of palladium bars, there are palladium coins such as the Palladium Canadian Maple Leaf.

Note about liquidity / tradability of coins: There is a well-established network of more than 5,000 "coin shops" in the United States that provide excellent buy/sell markets for both rare coins and bullion coins. These shops, large and small, are in addition to the big online and national dealers that advertise on radio and television. The point is that you have many options when you own precious metals in the event you want to cash out for dollars or to pay off a loan when the metals prices go sky-high.

After reading this book, including Appendices A, B and C, you can get updated spot prices and coin prices per our Model Precious Metals Portfolios at our website: www.WashingtonGoldExchange.com. The website also has many in-depth articles about precious metals, how to store them, etc. Also, check out my sister's website for a myriad of articles, including many about history and law: www.YouShouldBuyGold.com.

If you have any questions, or if you want to receive our newsletter, you can call our 24-hour Hotline and leave a message at (206) 719-6368. I will get back to you during regular business hours: Monday through Friday, 8 am to 5 pm (Pacific Time). Or you can email me at any time: craig@ washingtongoldexchange.com.

$10,000 in gold and silver coins purchased 9/10/2015;
Now worth $11,880 (September, 2017).
See Model Precious Metals Portfolios in Appendix B.

Teach Your Children (and Grandchildren) about Money

You have a moral obligation to teach your children and grandchildren about saving, thrift, budgeting and honest weights and measures. With wealth comes responsibility, and our country is in trouble financially because parents and schools- since about 1950 - have avoided teaching the virtues of frugality and saving. We have lived beyond our means and many parents who went through the Great Depression wanted their children to have what they didn't have. So they gave their children too much, with little training about money and the pitfalls of debt.

In our schools, we were taught Keynesian economics - that we could systematically debase our currency through the creation of paper money and credit (without gold backing) - and this artificial stimulation of the economy would result in prosperity. This thinking permeated our personal lives and - over time - resulted in less and less personal responsibility in family budgets. Is it any wonder that federal, state and local budgets keep growing exponentially? Most of our elected representatives have learned that it's OK to spend beyond your means, and this has led to a federal debt of much more than $20 TRILLION.

A client of mine sent me a cute story about his granddaughter Zoe that provides an excellent example of what we need to do to teach important lessons about money to our children:

"Several years ago I decided to teach my granddaughter the value of paper money relative to hard currency. I reached into my pocket and pulled out a crisp new five dollar bill and an old silver dollar.

"Zoe, which of these pieces of money would you rather have?" Not to my surprise she reached for the $5 dollar bill. "Wait a minute Zoe, let's talk about ice cream cones." She looked at her crazy grandpa and nodded in agreement.

"When I was your age a paper dollar and a silver dollar were of equal value. Both of them would buy me 20 ice cream cones. "Zoe, how much does an ice cream cone cost now? She replied, 'About a dollar and a half.'

"Do you know how many you could buy with the silver dollar you chose <u>not</u> to accept? Zoe: 'No. How many?'

"You could still buy twenty.

"Her eyes lit up. She understood, even at the tender age of twelve. 'Grandpa, Can I exchange the five dollar bill for the silver dollar?'

"I'm no hard-hearted Hanna, so of course I handed it over. My point had been made. Now, whenever we get together, she receives more silver and a short discussion on inflation, devaluation of paper currency and the like.

"And as you might imagine, I have set aside precious metals for her education."

Bravo! My client (and friend) has and continues to teach his grand-daughter important life lessons. I urge you to do the same with your children and grandchildren. A good way to start conversations about money and to teach them life lessons is to give silver and gold coins to them for birthdays, Christmas, or graduation. Then follow up with dialogue about what they have received, encouraging them to save, not spend.

In 1991, my wife and I developed Monthly Money: Allowance & Responsibility System for Kids & Teenagers. We published two kits that included a Parents' Manual, recommended allowances and it included an agreement signed by the child that he or she would do required chores around the home. It also included a planning book and a vinyl portfolio with six resealable pockets for the child to keep money allocated as follows: 10% for Charity; 10% for Savings; 20% for Clothing; 40% for Spending; 10% for Gifts; and 10% for Miscellaneous. A few copies are still available at Amazon.

Visit *RhynesGuide.com* to:

- *Setup a FREE 30-minute consultation with Craig Rhyne*
- *Sign up for monthly e-newsletters*
- *Order more books*
- *Access video reports*
- *Live chat: (206) 719-6368*

Rhyne - Buswell
Family Lore about Gold and Silver

MY FAMILY HISTORY has impacted me greatly - both spiritually and materially. My mother's ninth great-grandfather, Giles Badger, came from England and settled in Newbury, Massachusetts in 1635. In his will, Giles wrote: "I give and bqueathe my soule to God and my body to the earth to be buried in hope to be raised againe in the resurrection by Jesus Christ my savior...." Giles and his wife, Elizabeth, left a legacy that includes Mary Badger, who married Caleb Buswell, my fifth great-grandfather in 1760. Caleb signed the Association Test at Concord, New Hampshire, in 1776 and is one of my "Patriot Ancestors" as a member of Sons of the American Revolution (SAR).

Jacob Rein (Rhyne), another fifth great-grandfather, arrived in the American colonies in 1738 after a long trip from Blankenloch, Germany. He and his family settled in York, Pennsylvania. He married Elizabeth Glatfelder in 1750 at Christ Lutheran Evangelical Church in York. Jacob and Elizabeth and the first of their children moved to North Carolina in 1764 to settle land owned by Elizabeth's brother and uncle. Jacob was a provisioner of the troops who fought in the American Revolutionary War, and is another "Patriot Ancestor."

Moving ahead to 1914…Wallace Eugene Buswell, my mother Nelma's father, sought his fortune mining gold at Ester Creek near Fairbanks, Alaska. Grandpa Buswell met my Finnish grandmother, Ina, at a dance in 1915, then married her and had Aunt Ellen and Aunt Wilma in Alaska. (Ina had emigrated from Finland, traveling through Canada to Fairbanks, to work for her Aunt and Uncle Gius in their boarding house.) After coming back from Alaska in 1917 with $6,500 in gold (when gold was $20 per ounce) to Portland, Oregon, my mother and Uncle Anor were born. In 1921, Wallace and Ina moved to Toledo, Washington to buy farm property and build a home. The capital used to do this came from what he received for the Alaska gold, estimated to be 325 ounces. Uncle Don and Aunt Hazel were born in their Toledo home and Uncle Don and Aunt Bernice still live there.

In 1970…my father, Alfred Avery Rhyne, died (too soon) in Forks, Washington, leaving his wife, my mother, Nelma, and our family a trucking business, Atlas Trucking Company. (This business continues today in Port Angeles under new owners.) Only months after Dad's funeral, a friend of mine told me about a book by Dr. Harry Browne, How to Profit from the Coming Devaluation. In the book, Dr. Browne made a compelling case that the dollar would continue to lose purchasing power, and that silver (then at $1.29 per ounce) and gold (at $40 per ounce) should be purchased to protect a family estate. He said that at least 10% of one's assets should be put into physical gold and silver, and possibly, into Swiss Franc currency.

Based on this advice, and since our family succeeded in selling the business (yielding a tidy sum of cash), I guided my mother and siblings to purchase 1,000 British Sovereign gold coins (.2354 oz gold) for $10.65 each. I also succeeded in having her purchase twenty $1,000 "junk silver bags" of pre-1965 dimes, quarter and half-dollars. The purchases were timely, especially as the gold and silver prices have since doubled, tripled, quadrupled and much more. (The price of gold today is more than 33 times what it was in 1970.) Needless to say, the experience profoundly affected me and provided me a sense of calling for my life.

My life took a major turn in 1972 that resulted in my purchase of leveraged positions in silver (at $2 per ounce). I had lost my left leg (just above the knee) in an auto accident caused by a drunk driver. There was $25,000 in insurance paid to my attorneys, and after their take, I got $19,000. This is what I invested in silver, and then it more than doubled in two years. I founded C. Rhyne & Associates in 1974, at age 24, in Tacoma, WA. My "leg money" was the seed money to start the company. Needless to say, the purchases of gold and silver - as a result of my father's death and the loss of my leg - profoundly affected me. In fact, they linked me emotionally to a sense of calling for my life.

The company philosophy centered on the economic principles of the "free market" and the "Austrian school of economics." (Also known as the "gold school," as expounded in the writings of Ludwig von Mises and Hans Sennholz.) Practically speaking, I would often tell prospective clients about how I could buy a fine wool man's suit with $20, *as long as it was an old $20 gold piece minted before 1933*. (Today these coins sell for about $1,344 in Almost Uncirculated condition, which will buy a very fine suit!)

I moved the business to Pioneer Square in Seattle in 1976, the same year I met Faith Richardson. My sister, Denise, was my first receptionist and her role expanded to salesperson, eventually opening the Rhyne Gold Salon with coin jewelry and exquisite high-karat gold chains, diamonds and gems. (Denise and our mother were key to the success of my business and now Denise writes prolifically about history, education, geopolitical developments, and about precious metals. See her website: YouShouldBuyGold.com.)

Faith and I married in 1977; then a few months later we learned that Faith was expecting, and we got caught up in the natural birth movement. Curiously, Faith and I found a medical doctor, Morris Gold, MD, who owned the Lynnwood Clinic with his wife, Barbara. Before our oldest son's birth, now 39 years ago, Dr. Gold and I negotiated his fee in terms of gold coins, in fact, using British Sovereign gold coins that our family purchased in 1970. Gold had moved up to $211 at the time, so each Sovereign was worth $52. I paid Dr. Gold four of these coins, which covered his personal medical care, and the entire cost of the clinic and the follow-up. (The $200 fee wasn't increased even though Faith was in labor for 32 hours and there was no hospital charge.) Today, those Sovereigns would be worth about $316 each, for a total of $1,264. Dr. Gold really liked the barter exchange, and so did I, especially since our family first bought the Sovereigns for $10.65 each. It was a very satisfying experience!

British Gold Sovereign coin
("one pound Sterling," .2354 T. oz gold)

In 1980 we were blessed with a daughter; and a second son was born in 1983. Both were born in our family home with the assistance of a Swedish midwife.

Needless to say, I have family history on both my mother's and father's sides involving gold and silver. This has informed my life work in a profound way. While it has never been easy to be in the gold business (especially since it has been counter to regular investments), I am fortunate to have known exactly what I must do.

About the Author

I grew up in western Washington State and graduated in Business Administration from the University of Washington. I founded C. Rhyne & Associates in 1974, Rhyne Precious Metals in 1986 and Washington Gold Exchange in 2009. I have served more than twenty thousand investors throughout the United States. Besides co-founding state and national trade associations, I led the effort to eliminate the sales tax on precious metals and coins in Washington State. The result was elimination of Washington State sales and use tax on investment coins and bars in 1985, saving investors millions of dollars, allowing local businesses to compete with out-of-state dealers, and offering consumers greater protection by dealing face-to-face rather than sending money to dealers in other states.

WA State Governor Booth Gardner signing the bill eliminating sales tax on precious metals and rare coins in 1985. Standing at left, the key players were Mark Gjurasic (lobbyist), myself, and Lee Sanders.

Over the last 40 years, I have counseled thousands of people, transacted hundreds of millions of dollars of business, and educated thousands about American history, good government, and sound money. I created and developed "Monthly Money" kits in 1991 to help parents teach their children about money and responsibility. Besides enjoying three children and six grandchildren, I sing in choirs, serve on the board of the Asian Pacific Children's Fund, and am active in Rotary International. I am keenly interested in American history and serve as the Chairman of the America's Founding Documents committee of the Sons of the American Revolution. I will never retire - until my Maker calls me home.

Craig W. Rhyne

Visit *RhynesGuide.com* to:

- *Setup a FREE 30-minute consultation with Craig Rhyne*
- *Sign up for monthly e-newsletters*
- *Order more books*
- *Access video reports*
- *Live chat: (206) 719-6368*

Acknowledgements, Qualifications and Research Sources

Many thanks to the following friends who helped me gather price history information, clarify certain points, or critically review my text: Philip Beyers, Dr. Robert Bockoven, Richard Calkins, Nancy Christel, Glenn Dobbs, Steve Entin, Dr. John Stieber, and Michael Weinstein. Further, my sister Denise has done excellent research and written succinctly about history, law, education, theology, organizations, governments, power, and precious metals, which I have relied on extensively. (Her website: www.YouShouldBuyGold.com)

The technical and price data presented here, particularly information about bartering, taxes, and other transactions - as well as the law, legal information, and methods of exchanging personal property - reflect my individual beliefs and experiences under specific circumstances and these may not apply to the reader.

The information in this book should therefore be used for guidance only and approached with caution; advice for the reader's specific circumstances and tax implications should be obtained from a lawyer or other expert. Neither the author nor the publisher assumes any responsibility for the use or misuse of information contained in this book.

Price information in Appendix C has been gleaned through online databases, libraries and online research from many sources, including government organizations, in-store visits and interviews. Examples: Wage amounts are from the Social Security Administration; Home sale prices are from the Federal Reserve Bank of St. Louis. Energy prices have come from the U.S. Energy Information Administration. We have used many media reports comparing costs over the decades. With many gaps in the data, we have had to estimate and make projections for some items. Overall, while we cannot prove many of the amounts, we have done our best to provide the most accurate information.

Many thanks to Dillon Gage Metals Division for many of the coin photographs in Appendix A, as well as coin specifications, Grading and Condition descriptions, and definitions for the Glossary of Terms. Also, thanks to Anne Hilling and Brian Williams of Hilling Design for various photos. Finally, I appreciate the encouragement given to me by Richard Geasey to write this book.

Unless where noted, prices for gold, silver, platinum are in Troy ounces, and the price indications for coins were as of September 1, 2017, when gold was $1,326, silver was $17.75 and platinum was $1,009. Also, the photographs of the coins and bars do not show them actual size.

Note: My sister Denise has written an excellent article **Buying Gold & Silver Coins & Bars.** Go to her website, www.YouShouldBuyGold.com and click on the Gold & Silver tab just below "Things You Probably Didn't Learn in School." The article starts on page 24 and ends on page 27.

Visit RhynesGuide.com to:

- *Setup a FREE 30-minute*
- *consultation with Craig Rhyne*
- *Signup for insightful e-newsletters*
- *Order more books*
- *Access video reports*
- *Live chat: (206) 719-6368*

$1 Million purchased by a client 9/10/2015, Now worth $1.189 Million two years later. The yellow and green boxes are "monster boxes" containing tubes of 1 oz Silver Maple Leafs or American Silver Eagles. See Model Precious Metals Portfolios in Appendix B.

Appendices

Appendix A - Best Coins for Barter - Tier I, Silver I

Prices are indications only based on silver at $17.75 per ounce.

The "first step" you should take is to get real SILVER coins (or small bars) so you have a medium of exchange for "small items," such as a gallon of water or a loaf of bread:

All precious metals weights are in Troy oz.

Price updates: www.WashingtonGoldExchange.com

Old, pre-1965 U.S. Dimes, Quarters and Half-dollars

Recommended per family: At least one $1,000 face bag (delivered in two half-bags, about 27 lbs. each). Because they are circulated, there is a slight loss from wear with resulting silver contents:

Dime: 0.9715 oz silver; Quarter: 0.17875 oz; Half-dollar: 0.3573 oz. (Kennedy half-dollars minted 1965 through 1969 are 40% silver.)

A "bag" of old dimes has 10,000 coins and approx. 715 oz pure silver. A bag of quarters contains 4,000 quarters; a bag of halves has 2,000 coins. 1/10, 1/4, and 1/2 bag sizes available. Cost of full "bag" ($1,000 face) on September 1, 2017: $13,520

Old, pre-1936 U.S. Morgan or Peace Silver Dollars (circulated, VF to XF, possibly AU)

Morgan Silver Dollars were minted from 1878 to 1904, and in 1921. Silver content: 0.77344 oz Circulated coins, VF to AU, range from $21 to $34.

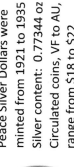

Peace Silver Dollars were minted from 1921 to 1935 Silver content: 0.77344 oz Circulated coins, VF to AU, range from $18 to $22.

Appendix A - Best Coins for Barter - Tier I, Silver II

In addition to the old U.S. silver coins, there are fine options for 1 oz silver coins issued by the United States, Australia, Austria, and Canada. All are .999 fine silver (no alloy), except for some from Australia and Canada. Prices are indications only based on silver at $17.75 per ounce.

American Eagle 1 oz Silver Eagle (.999 fine)

Minted 1986 and every year since.

Dia.: 40.6 mm   Thickness: 2.98 mm

Austrian 1 oz Silver Philharmonic (.999 fine)

Diameter: 37 mm
Thickness: 3.2 mm
These and all the 1 oz silver coins can be purchased in tubes, or in boxes of 500 (coins in tubes). Currently, about $19.50 each.

Australian Silver Kangaroo, Koala, or Kookaburra

(.999, .9995, or .9999 fine)

Minted since 1990.

Sizes: 1/10, 1/4, 1/2, 1, 2, 10, Kilo
1 oz coins diameter: 32.6 to 40.6 r
1 oz Coins Thickness: 4 to 6 mm
Mint box of 250 1 oz at right.
Silver Eagles and these
Australian coins
sell for about $20 each.

Canadian 1 oz Silver Maple Leaf (.9999 fine)

Diameter: 31.11 mm
Thickness: 3.29 mm
First minted in 1988, they have been minted every year since and are the biggest competitor of the American Eagle. Currently, about $19.50 ea.

Appendix A - Best Coins for Barter - Tier I, Silver III

Besides the Silver Brittania, Mexico produces Silver Libertads in 8 sizes: 1/20, 1/10, 1/4, 1/2, 1, 2, 5, and 1 Kilogram.

Also, there are 1/10, 1/4, 1/2 and 1 oz silver "rounds" produced by several fine private mints, all .999 fine silver.

Prices are indications only based on silver at $17.75 per ounce.

British 1 oz Silver Britannia (.958 to .999 fine)

Minted by Royal Mint since 1997.

Diameter:

40 mm up to 2012
38.61 in 2013 +
in 2013 and later.

Thickness: 3 mm

Come in tubes
of 25 coins.

Currently,
about $19.50
each coin.

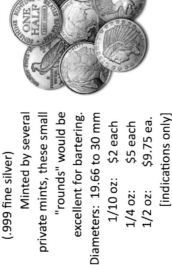

1/10, 1/4, and 1/2 oz Silver Rounds compare to 90% Silver coins

(.999 fine silver)

Minted by several
private mints, these small
"rounds" would be
excellent for bartering.

Diameters: 19.66 to 30 mm

1/10 oz:	$2 each
1/4 oz:	$5 each
1/2 oz:	$9.75 ea.

[indications only]

Sunshine Silver 1 oz Round (.999 fine)

Diameter: 38.5 mm

Thickness: 2.8 mm

Rounds come in
tubes / boxes of
500. Save about
one dollar per oz
compared to "coins."

Currently, about $19 each

Silver Buffalo 1 oz Round (.999 fine)

Diameter: 39.3 mm

Thickness: 3.2 mm

Rounds come in
tubes / boxes of
500. Save about
one dollar per oz
compared to "coins."

Currently, about $19 each

Appendix A - Best Coins for Barter - Tier I, Gold I

American Eagle Gold Coins (United States Mint)

In addition to silver, which will be handy for bartering for "small things," you will want gold coins. When the price of gold hits $5,000 or higher, it will be awfully nice to have some fractional gold coins, such as 1/20, 1/10, 1/4, or 1/2 ounce coins. Also, it will be easier to barter with coins that have exact weights stamped on them.

1/10 oz Gold American Eagle ($5 denomination)

Minted since 1986; 22K (.916 fine)

Total weight: .1091 oz (3.393 grams)

Diameter: 16.5 mm

Come in tubes of 50
Currently, $149 each coin
Tube of 50: $7,450

1/4 oz Gold American Eagle ($10 denomination)

Minted since 1986; 22K (.916 fine)

Total weight: .272 oz (8.482 grams)

Diameter: 22 mm

Come in tubes of 40. Currently, $365 each. Tube of 40: $14,600

1/2 oz Gold American Eagle ($25 denomination)

Minted since 1986; 22K (.916 fine)

Total weight: .5455 oz (16.966 grams)

Diameter: 27 mm

Come in tube of 40
Currently, $713 ea.
Tube - 40: $28,520

1 oz Gold American Eagle ($50 denomination)

Minted since 1986; 22K (.916 fine)

Total weight: 1.0910 oz (33.933 grams)

Diameter: 32.7 mm

Come in tube of 20
Currently: $1,386
Tube - 20: $27,720

Prices are indications only based on gold at $1,326.

Appendix A - Best Coins for Barter - Tier I, Gold II

Canadian Gold Maple Leaf

These beautiful coins come in standard weight sizes: 1 oz, 1/2, 1/4, 1/10, 1/20 oz and 1 Gram. Since Canada is a friendly neighbor, there is a natural trust of their coins. Also, their coins are not alloyed, making them more attractive to Asian investors who like 24K.

Prices are indications only based on gold at $1,326.

1 Gram Gold Canadian Maple Leaf (25 per packet)

Minted since 2016; 24K (.9999 fine)

Weight: 1 Gram

(.0322 oz)

Diameter: 8 mm

9/1/2017: $49 ea.

25 / pack: $1,225

1/10 oz Gold Canadian Maple Leaf ($5 denomination)

Minted since 1982; 24K (.9999 fine)

Weight: .1 Troy oz (3.1103 grams)

Diameter: 16 mm

9/1/2017: $147

1/4 oz Gold Canadian Maple Leaf ($10 denomination)

Minted since 1982; 22K (.916 fine)

Weight: .25 oz (7.7758 grams)

Diameter: 20 mm

9/1/2017: $360

1/2 oz Gold Canadian Maple Leaf ($20 denomination)

Minted since 1986; 24K (.9999 fine)

Weight: .5 oz (15.551 grams)

Diameter: 25 mm

9/1/2017: $705

1 oz Gold Canadian Maple Leaf ($50 denomination)

Minted since 1979; 24K (.9999 fine)

Weight: 1 Troy oz (31.1033 grams)

Diameter: 30 mm

Tubes of 10 or 20

9/1/2017: $1,378 ea.

Tube of 10: $13,780

Appendix A - Best Coins for Barter - Tier I, Gold III

Old U.S. $5, $10, and $20 Gold Pieces

We have included old U.S. gold pieces in circulated condition in Tier I, but not rare dates/high grades/certified coins. Low costs for these circulated coins (VF to AU) makes them comparable to the exact weight modern coins.

Prices are indications only based on gold at $1,326.

Old $5 Liberty Head Gold Piece ("Half-Eagle")

Minted 1866 to 1907; 21.6K (.900 fine)

Weight: .26875 oz (8.3592 grams) Diameter: 21 mm

Fine Gold Content: .2419 oz (7.5233 grams)

XF Grade
9/1/2017: $357

Old $10 Liberty Head Gold Piece ("Eagle")

Minted 1866 to 1907; 21.6K (.900 fine)

Weight: .5375 oz (16.7185 grams) Diameter: 27 mm

Fine Gold Content: .4838 oz (15.0466 grams)

XF Grade
9/1/2017: $700

Old $20 Liberty Head Gold Piece ("Double Eagle")

Minted 1907 to 1933; 21.6K (.900 fine)

Weight: 1.075 Troy oz (33.4370 grams) Dia.: 34 mm

Fine Gold Content: .9675 oz (30.0933 grams)

AU Grade
9/1/17
$1,390 each

Old $20 St. Gaudens Gold Piece ("Double Eagle")

Minted 1907 to 1933; 21.6K (.900 fine)

Weight: 1.075 Troy oz (33.4370 grams) Diameter: 34 mm

Fine Gold Content: .9675 oz (30.0933 grams)

AU Grade
9/1/17
$1,395 each

Not pictured are the higher premium old U.S. $10 Indian, $5 and smaller denominations, which are listed on page 89

Appendix A - Best Coins for Barter - Tier I and II, Gold IV

U.S. Buffalo, Krugerrands, Australian Kangaroo, Austrian Philharmonic

Minted by the U.S. Mint, the Buffalo is 24K gold (not 21.6K like the other American coins).

The venerable Krugerrand is a great option, as well as Australian Kangaroos and Austrian Philharmonics.

Prices are indications only based on gold at $1,326.

1 oz Gold American Buffalo

Only 1 oz - minted since 2006; 24K (.9999 fine)

Weight: 1 Troy oz (31.1033 grams) Dia: 32.7 mm

Buffalo
9/1/17
$1,393 ea.

1 oz South African Krugerrand

Minted 1967 to present; 22K (.916 fine)

Weight: 1.0909 oz (33.933 grams) Dia.: 32.6 mm

Available in 1/10,
1/4, 1/2 and 1 oz.
See next page.

9/1/17
1 oz: $1,379

Australian Kangaroo, 1/20 to 1 Kilo (8 sizes)

Minted 1989 to present; 24K (.9999 fine)

Weights and Sizes: See chart on next page.

Austrian Philharmonic, 1/25, 1/10, 1/4, 1/2 and 1 oz

Minted 1989 to present; 24K (.9999 fine)

Appendix A - Best Coins for Barter - Tier II, Gold V

Tier I and II coins are the best for barter because their gold weights are stamped on them, and they come in standard fractional sizes. Chinese Pandas come in 24K in five standard sizes, but they usually have high premiums. * Note that Krugerrands weigh 10% more than their gold contents because the gold in them is alloyed with copper for hardness.

Prices are indications only based on gold at $1,326.

	Denom.	Minted Since	Total Weight	Diameter	Thickness	Fineness	Price
Krugerrand (4 sizes)*							
1/10 oz Krugerrand	No face	1980	3.393 grams	16.55 mm	1.35 mm	22K (.9167 fine)	$147
1/4 oz Krugerrand	values.	1980	8.482 grams	22.06 mm	1.888 mm	22K (.9167 fine)	$360
1/2 oz Krugerrand		1980	16.965 grams	27.07 mm	2.215 mm	22K (.9167 fine)	$704
1 oz Krugerrand		1967	33.930 grams	32.77 mm	2.84 mm	22K (.9167 fine)	$1,379
Kangaroo (8 sizes)							
1/20 oz Kangaroo	$5 Aus.	1989	1.5552 grams	14.1 mm	1.4 mm	24K (.9999 fine)	$80
1/10 oz Kangaroo	$15 Aus.	1989	3.1103 grams	16.1 mm	1.3 mm	24K (.9999 fine)	$147
1/4 oz Kangaroo	$25 Aus.	1989	7.776 grams	20.1 mm	1.8 mm	24K (.9999 fine)	$360
1/2 oz Kangaroo	$50 Aus.	1989	15.551 grams	25.1 mm	2.2 mm	24K (.9999 fine)	$704
1 oz Kangaroo	$100 Aus	1989	31.103 grams	32.6 mm	2.8 mm	24K (.9999 fine)	$1,382
2 oz Kangaroo	$200 Aus	1989	62.206 grams	40.6 mm	4 mm	24K (.9999 fine)	$2,900
10 oz Kangaroo	$1,000 A	1989	311.035 grams	60.3 mm	7.9 mm	24K (.9999 fine)	$13,800
1 Kilogram Kangaroo	$3,000 A	1989	1,000 grams	75.6 mm	13.9 mm	24K (.9999 fine)	$43,800
Philharmonic (5 sizes)							
1/25 oz Philharmonic	4 €	2014	1.2441 grams	13 mm	.92 mm	24K (.9999 fine)	$70
1/10 oz Philharmonic	10 €	1991	3.1103 grams	16 mm	1.2 mm	24K (.9999 fine)	$147
1/4 oz Philharmonic	25 €	1989	7.776 grams	22 mm	1.2 mm	24K (.9999 fine)	$360
1/2 oz Philharmonic	50 €	1994	15.55175 grams	28 mm	1.6 mm	24K (.9999 fine)	$704
1 oz Philharmonic	100 €	1989	31.1035 grams	37 mm	2 mm	24K (.9999 fine)	$1,386

The Austrian Mint produced a 20 ounce Philharmonic in 2009, but the coin is not suitable for barter because of its size.

Appendix A - Best Coins for Barter - Tier I and II, Gold VI

These British and Chinese coins also come in convenient sizes; however, they have higher premiums.

British Britannia (British Royal Mint)
Minted since 1987; 24K (.9999 fine)

Size	Denom.	Diameter	Thickness	Weight; Net Gold	Price
1/20 oz	1 £	12 mm	.83 mm	1.5552 grams	$82
1/10 oz	10 £	16.5 mm	1.8 mm	3.1104 grams	$156
1/4 oz	25 £	22 mm	1.63 mm	7.776 grams	$374
1/2 oz	50 £	27 mm	2.08 mm	16.05175 grams	$720
1 oz	100 £	32.69 mm	1.8 mm	31.1035 grams	$1,380

Prices are indications only based on gold at $1,326.

In 2016, the **China Mint** replaced the fractional ounce coins with coins weighing exact numbers of grams, matching the Metric system.

Size	Denom.	Diameter	Thickness	Gold in Troy oz	Price
1 Gram	10 Yuan	10 mm	.83 mm	0.03215	$38
3 Gram	50 Yuan	18 mm	1.05 mm	0.09645	$165
8 Gram	100 Yuan	22 mm	1.53 mm	0.25721	$385
15 Gram	200 Yuan	27 mm	1.85 mm	0.48226	$694
30 Gram	500 Yuan	32 mm	2.70 mm	0.96452	$1,430

Size	Denom.	Diameter	Thickness	Gold in Grams	Price
1/20 oz	Varies by	13.92 mm	.83 mm	1.5552 grams	$97
1/10 oz	year	17.95 mm	1.05 mm	3.1104 grams	$173
1/4 oz	from 10	21.95 mm	1.53 mm	7.776 grams	$379
1/2 oz	to 500	27 mm	1.85 mm	15.55175 grams	$718
1 oz	Yuan	32.1 mm	2.7 mm	31.1035 grams	$1,461

Chinese Panda
Minted since 1982; 24K (.999 fine)

Most high-grade numismatic coins would not maintain their high premiums in a "barter environment." However, many prefer the old U.S. coins - in lower grades - because they are so old. Also, the last five (modern issues) have very low premiums.

use the information below to determine their values. Also, the last five (modern issues) have low premiums.

	Type	Dated	Total Weight	Diameter	Thickness	Fineness	Net Gold Troy oz.	*Price AU qual.
$1.00 Gold Piece	Type I	1849-1854	1.6718 grams	13 mm	1.02 mm	0.9000	0.0483	$215
$1.00 Gold Piece	Type III	1856-1889	1.6718 grams	15 mm	.76 mm	0.9000	0.0483	$230
$2.50 Gold Piece	Liberty	1840-1907	4.1769 grams	18.2 mm	1.27 mm	0.9000	0.1209	$352
$2.50 Gold Piece	Indian	1908-1929	4.1769 grams	18.2 mm	1.27 mm	0.9000	0.1209	$302
$5 Gold Piece "Half Eagle"	Liberty	1866-1908	8.3592 grams	21.6 mm	1.59 mm	0.9000	0.2419	$388
$5 Gold Piece "Half Eagle"	Indian	1908-1929	8.3592 grams	21.6 mm	1.59 mm	0.9000	0.2419	$455
$10 Gold Piece "Eagle"	Liberty	1866-1907	16.7185 grams	27 mm	2.03 mm	0.9000	0.4838	$740
$10 Gold Piece "Eagle"	Indian	1907-1933	16.7185 grams	27 mm	2.03 mm	0.9000	0.4838	$800
$20 Gold Pc. "Double Eagle"	Liberty	1877-1907	33.4370 grams	34 mm	2.41 mm	0.9000	0.9675	$1,398
$20 Gold Pc. "Double Eagle"	St. Gaud.	1907-1933	33.4370 grams	34 mm	2.41 mm	0.9000	0.9675	$1,403
*1 oz U.S. Arts Medallion	BU	1980-1984	34.5594 grams	32.2 mm	3 mm	0.9000	1.00	$1,370
**1/2 oz U.S. Arts Medaln.	BU	1980-84	17.2797 grams	27.5 mm	2 mm	0.9000	0.50	$684
1/2 oz U.S. First Spouse	BU	Since 2007	15.5517 grams	26.49 mm	1.88 mm	0.9999	0.50	$720
$5 U.S. Commemorative	BU	Since 1986	8.3589 grams	21.6 mm	1.75 mm	0.9000	0.2419	$350
$10 U.S. Commemorative	BU	Since 1984	16.718 grams	27 mm	2.2 mm	0.9000	0.4838	$700

Prices are indications only based on gold at $1,326.

Prices for pre-1934 gold pieces assume Almost Uncirculated (AU) condition, based on the 9/1/2017 price of gold, $1,326. The Type II $1 Gold Piece and $3 Gold Pieces are not shown because they are rare. For barter, with the very old coins, buy the better priced circulated grades (VF, XF, AU). *1 oz, per year: G. Wood, M. Twain, L. Armstrong, R. Frost, H. Hayes
** 1/2 oz, per year: M. Anderson, W. Cather, F. Wright, A. Calder, J. Steinbeck

Appendix A - Best Coins for Barter - Tier III, Gold VIII

Prices indications only based on gold at $1,326.

Tier I & II coins are best for barter because they are exact fractional sizes and have gold contents stamped on them. However, these Tier III coins are well-known; use the information below to calculate values.

	Details	Dated	Total Weight	Diameter	Thickness	Fineness	Net Gold Troy oz.	Price
Austrian 1 Ducat	Restrike	1915	3.4909 grams	19.6 mm	.8 mm	0.9867	0.1107	$160
Austrian 4 Ducat	Restrike	1915	13.9636 grams	39.5 mm	.7 mm	0.9867	0.4489	$613
*Austrian/Hung. 10 Corona	Restrike	1915	3.3875 grams	19 mm	.9 mm	0.9000	0.09802	$140
*Austrian/Hung. 20 Corona	Restrike	1915	6.7751 grams	21 mm	1.4 mm	0.9000	0.19604	$280
*Austr./Hung. 100 Corona	Restrike	1915	33.8753 grams	37 mm	2.3 mm	0.9000	0.9802	$1,330
**British Gold Sovereign	1 Pound	Since 1871	7.9881 grams	22 mm	1.52 mm	0.9167	0.2354	$325
Chilean 100 Peso	Original	1926-1980	20.3397 grams	31.1 mm	2.1 mm	0.9000	0.5885	$868
Colombian 5 Peso	Original	1919-1930	7.9881 grams	22 mm	1.5 mm	0.9167	0.2354	$330
Dutch 10 Guilders	Original	1911-33	6.729 grams	22.3 mm	1.3 mm	0.9000	0.1947	$270
***French 10 Francs	Original	1854-1860	3.2258 grams	19 mm	.8 mm	0.9000	0.09334	$148
*** French 20 Francs	Original	1861-1915	6.4516 grams	21 mm	1.4 mm	0.9000	0.1867	$260
German 20 Mark	Original	1894-1914	7.9650 grams	22 mm	1.5 mm	0.9000	0.2305	$330
Italian 20 Lira	Original	1861-1897	6.4516 grams	21 mm	1.3 mm	0.9000	0.1867	$260
Russian 5 Rouble	Original	1897-1911	4.3013 grams	18.6 mm	1.2 mm	0.9000	0.1245	$240
Russian Chervonetz	10 Rouble	1975-1982	8.6026 grams	22.6 mm	1.6 mm	0.9000	0.2489	$415
***Swiss 20 Franc (Vrenelli)	Original	1897-1949	6.4516 grams	21 mm	1.4 mm	0.9000	0.1867	$260
Uruguayan 5 Peso	Original	1930	8.4850 gram	22.3 mm	1.6 mm	0.9167	0.2501	$350

*Austro-Hungarian Empire produced gold coins of same specifications, e.g., Austrian and Hungarian 10 Corona (Korona); Austrian and Hungarian 20 Corona (Korona); and Austrian and Hungarian 100 Corona (Korona); same prices.

** British Sovereigns: 7 designs featuring Victoria, Edward VII, George V, and Elizabeth II. *** French 20 Francs in three types: Napoleon, Angel and Rooster. Many other possibilities, e.g., Swiss 10 Francs (same gold content as French 10 Franc).

Appendix A - Mexican Gold Coins, Tier III, Gold IX

Mexico has a long history (since 1535) of producing beautiful coins, including restrikes that pre-date Krugerrands, etc.

Mexican Gold Libertad / Onza Coins

1/4, 1/2 and 1 oz minted 1981, 83, 89 were 900 fine.

Since 1991, 1/20, 1/10, 1/4, 1/2, and 1 oz
have been 24K (.9999 fine)

Size	Diameter	Thickness	Weight; Net Gold	Price
1/20 oz	13 mm	.83 mm	1.5552 grams	$100
1/10 oz	16 mm	1 mm	3.1104 grams	$155
1/4 oz	23 mm	1.4 mm	7.776 grams	$365
1/2 oz	29 mm	1.75 mm	15.55175 grams	$715
1 oz	34.5 mm	1.8 mm	31.1035 grams	$1,400

1/4, 1/2 and 1 oz amounts are for 1991 and later coins.

Prices are indications only based on gold at $1,326.

For updated spot prices, go to www.WashingtonGoldExchange.com.

Mexican Gold Pesos - All 21.6K (.900 fine)

Official Government Restrikes

Denom.	Minted	Dia.	Thickness	Total Weight		Net Gold Troy oz.	Price
2 Peso	1945	13 mm	1.02 mm	.0536 oz	1.666 gm	0.04822	$73
2-1/2 Peso	1945	15.5 mm	.86 mm	.0670 oz	2.083 gm	0.0603	$88
5 Peso	1955	19 mm	1.14 mm	.1339 oz	4.1665 gm	0.12055	$170
10 Peso	1959	22.5 mm	1.4 mm	.2379 oz	8.333 gm	0.24111	$334
20 Peso	1959	27.5 mm	2.03 mm	.5358 oz	16.666 gm	0.48222	$668
50 Peso	1947	37.08 mm	2.69 mm	1.3396 oz	41.6666 gm	1.20565	$1,653

Centenario   The Mexican Mint produced the Centenario in 1921, commemorating
the 100th anniversary of indepence from Spain. Then, restarted production in 1943.

Appendix A - Gold Bars & Platinum, Tier IV

There are excellent small gold bars (including multi, break-apart packs); also, platinum coins and bars.

Small Gold Bars (various)
Major Refineries; 24K (.9999 fine)

Size	Mint	Per Sheet	Gold content	Price
1 gram	PAMP Suisse	25	.8025 oz total	$1,200
1 gram	Valcambi CombiBar	20	.643 oz total	$960
1 gram	Valcambi CombiBar	50	1.6075 oz total	$2,300
2.5 gram	Credit Suisse	w/card	.080375 oz	$123
5 gram	PAMP or Perth Mint	w/card	.1607 oz	$240
10 gram	Republic Refinery	w/card	.3215 oz	$450
20 gram	Engelhard	w/card	.643 oz	$885
1 oz	Argor-Heraeus	w/card	31.1035 grams	$1,360

Bars have serial numbers, most with assay cards / sealed in plastic.
These hallmarks are almost interchangeable; most sizes from all mints.
Price indications only - based on gold at $1,326; platinum $1,009.

There are platinum bars ranging from 1 gram to 10 ounces, including multi, break-apart packs as with gold above.

Platinum Coins and Bars, all .9995 fine
Various Countries / Private Mints

Size	Mint	Coin	Diameter	Price
1/20 oz	Australia	Made by Australia	13.9 to 14.1 mm	N/A
1/10 oz	Pobjoy	Canada, China, U.S.,	16 to 16.5 mm	$145
1/4 oz	China	Isle of Man, but not	20 to 22 mm	$300
1/2 oz	U.S.	all available now.	25 to 27 mm	$550
1 oz	*Austria	*Plat. Philharmonic	30 to 37 mm	$1,070

* Also, other 1 oz coins: American Eagle, Australian Koala, Canadian Maple Leaf, Chinese Panda, Isle of Man Noble.

B. Model Precious Metals Portfolios

$2,500	Each	Totals
$100 face U.S. 90% silver coins (1/10 bag)	$1,487	$1,487
(7) 1/10 oz Gold American Eagles	$150	$1,050
		Total: $2,537
$10,000		
$500 face U.S. 90% silver coins (1/2 bag)	$6,885	$6,885
(21) 1/10 oz Gold American Eagles	$150	$3,150
		Total: $10,035
$25,000		
(260) 1 oz Silver American Eagles	$20.85	$5,421
$500 face U.S. 90% silver coins (1/2 bag)	$6,885	$6,885
(19) 1/4 oz Gold American Eagles	$364	$6,916
(40) 1/10 oz Gold American Eagles	$150	$6,000
		Total: $25,222
$50,000		
(500) 1 oz Silver American Eagles	$20.70	$10,350
$1,000 face U.S. 90% silver coins (1 bag)	$13,520	$13,520
(10) 1/2 oz Gold American Eagles	$714	$7,140
(32) 1/4 oz Gold American Eagles	$364	$11,648
(50) 1/10 oz Gold American Eagles	$150	$7,500
Full silver "bag" delivered as two 1/2 bags.		Total: $50,158
$100,000		
(750) 1 oz Silver American Eagles	$20.65	$15,488
$2,000 face U.S. 90% silver coins (2 bags)	$13,420	$26,820
(10) 1 oz Gold American Eagles	$1,381	$13,810
(10) 1/2 oz Gold American Eagles	$712	$7,120
(58) 1/4 oz Gold American Eagles	$363	$21,054
(60) 1/10 oz Gold American Eagles	$149	$8,940
(5) U.S. Old $20 Gold Piece - AU Lib.	$1,390	$6,950
Two silver "bags" delivered as four 1/2 bags.		Total: $100,182

$250,000		
(1,500) 1 oz Silver American Eagles	$20.60	$30,900
$3,000 face U.S. 90% silver coins (3 bags)	$13,370	$40,110
(50) 1 oz Gold American Eagles	$1,378	$68,900
(20) 1/2 oz Gold American Eagles	$711	$14,220
(97) 1/4 oz Gold American Eagles	$362	$35,114
(150) 1/10 oz Gold American Eagles	$148	$22,200
(10) U.S. Old $20 Liberty Gold Piece - AU	$1,385	$13,850
(10) U.S. Old $20 St. Gaudens Gold - AU	$1,390	$13,900
(10) 1 oz Platinum Maple Leaf coins	$1,081	$10,810
Three silver "bags" delivered as six 1/2 bags.		Total: $250,004

$500,000		
(2,000) 1 oz Silver American Eagles	$20.54	$41,080
(1,000) 1 oz Canadian Silver Maple Leafs	$20.13	$20,130
$4,000 face U.S. 90% silver coins (4 bags)	$13,213	$52,852
(50) 1 oz Gold American Eagles	$1,376	$68,800
(50) 1 oz Gold Canadian Maple Leafs	$1,373	$68,650
(40) 1/2 oz Gold American Eagles	$710	$28,400
(120) 1/4 oz Gold American Eagles	$361	$43,320
(200) 1/10 oz Gold American Eagles	$147	$29,400
(200) 1/10 oz Gold Canadian Maple Leafs	$146	$29,200
(24) Old U.S. $20 Liberty Head - AU	$1,380	$33,120
(23) Old U.S. $20 St. Gaudens - AU	$1,385	$31,855
(50) 1 oz Platinum Maple Leafs	$1,078	$53,900
Four silver "bags" delivered as eight 1/2 bags.		$500,707

9/1/2017 prices; gold at $1,326; platinum at $1,009; silver at $17.75. For updates, go to www.WashingtonGoldExchange.com

C. Price History of Gold, Silver and 41 Items since 1970.

	1970	1990	2010	2020
GOLD per ounce	$35.94	$383.00	$1,224.00	$2,500.00
SILVER per ounce	$1.63	$4.83	$20.19	$100.00
	Prices above are the averages for the year.			Projected
	PRICES IN TERMS OF OUNCES OF GOLD OR SILVER IN YELLOW BELOW.			
FOOD & DRINK				
Apples per pound	$0.15	$0.75	$1.20	$1.44
Red Delicious	Two old 90% silver dimes will now buy TWO pounds of apples!			
Big Mac	$0.50	$2.50	$3.73	$5.30
McDonald's	Four 90% silver dimes now worth $5.76 pay for a Big Mac.			
Beer	$2.00	$5.00	$9.00	$14.50
Budweiser, 12-pack, cans	EIGHT quarters in 1970; Today - if silver quarters - ONLY FOUR!			
Bread	$0.25	$0.70	$2.00	$4.00
Loaf, high quality	One 90% silver quarter, now worth $3.60, still pays for a loaf of bread.			
Butter	$0.87	$1.99	$3.63	$4.50
Per Pound	Less than four quarters in 1970; today it's only TWO silver quarters.			
Coca Cola	$0.60	$1.80	$2.50	$3.00
6-pack, 12 oz cans	Cost was six dimes in 1970; Now the cost is just one silver quarter!			
Coffee	$0.91	$2.97	$4.16	$7.00
Per Pound	One silver dollar in 1970. Today, THREE pounds with that silver dollar.			
Coffee	$0.25	$1.01	$2.00	$2.50
Cup at restaurant	Now ten times higher than in 1970. But a silver quarter buys a Mocha.			
Eggs	$0.60	$1.00	$2.65	$2.00
Dozen, large	Six silver dimes are now worth more than $7 and buy 3 dozen Jumbo eggs.			
Meat	$0.82	$2.21	$4.53	$8.00
Bacon per pound	Eight old silver dimes now worth than $11 buy you 37% more bacon today.			
Meat	$0.70	$1.56	$2.38	$5.00
Hamburger per pound	Hamburger has gone down over the last 47 years - ONLY 4 SILVER DIMES!			
Meat	$0.59	$1.60	$2.50	$7.00
Pot Roast per pound	Six pre-1965 silver dimes (.429 oz Ag) are now worth $7 - the current cost!			
Milk	$0.62	$2.50	$3.00	$3.29
Per Gallon	Six old silver dimes are now worth $7, which will now buy TWO gallons!			
Oats	$0.69	$1.44	$2.15	$2.62
Per bushel, large lots	24 lb pail of Rolled Oats today is $26 (or 7 old silver quarters, $1.75 face).			
Oranges	$0.07	$0.57	$0.91	$2.00
Per pound	A pound of oranges cost 28 times as much today as it did in 1970!			
Potatoes	$0.09	$0.37	$0.60	$0.67
Per pound	Potatoes now cost seven times as much as in 1970.			
Soup, Tomato	$0.10	$0.34	$0.70	$1.79
10.5 oz can	Only 10 cents per can in 1970. Price hasn't changed if it's an old silver dime.			
CLOTHING				
Gym shoes	$5.00	$16.00	$65.00	$100.00
Pair Men's Nike	Cost: Five silver dollars in 1970; FOUR 90% circulated silver dollars today.			
Men's Jeans	$10.00	$30.00	$50.00	$60.00
Blue or Black	Ten silver dollars in 1970. Today, only THREE old 90% silver dollars!			
Men's Dress Shoes	$20.00	$125.00	$300.00	$400.00
Leather	These shoes costs about twenty times as much today compared to 1970.			
Men's Sport Coat	$30.00	$275.00	$795.00	$1,000.00
Wool Dress	A fine sport coat cost the same in 1970 as today IF PAID IN GOLD!			
Men's Wool Suit	$40.00	$175.00	$995.00	$1,595.00
Fine, Hickey Freeman	The cost hasn't changed in gold; Today the cost is one old $20 gold piece!			

	1970	1990	2010	2020
GOLD per ounce	$35.94	$383.00	$1,224.00	$2,500.00
SILVER per ounce	$1.63	$4.83	$20.19	$100.00
	Prices above are the averages for the year.			Projected
	PRICES IN TERMS OF OUNCES OF GOLD OR SILVER IN YELLOW BELOW.			
HOME & UTILITIES				
Apartment Rent (ave.)	$415.00	$571.00	$950.00	$1,323.00
Per month, incl. utilities	It took 12 ounces of gold for a month's rent in 1970; today it takes only one.			
Cable for TV, Internet,	$70.00	$160.00	$200.00	$250.00
Phone (monthly)	Two ounces of gold per month in 1970; today it costs only 1/5 of one ounce.			
Electricty,	$0.022	$0.078	$0.120	$0.130
cents per Kilowatt/Hr.	Electricity is about six times higher in dollars today compared to 1970.			
Natural Gas,	$1.09	$5.80	$11.39	$10.94
Dollars per 1,000 cu. Feet	Natural gas costs ten times as much now as it did in 1970.			
Mattress and springs	$75.00	$150.00	$600.00	$1,000.00
	2 oz gold for a mattress/springs 47 years ago. Today, it's less than 1 ounce.			
Recliner chair, Leather	$70.00	$250.00	$260.00	$300.00
	Furniture rose less than most items because most is of poor quality from ?			
Home, average sale price	$26,000.00	$150,000.00	$270,000.00	$406,000.00
	723 oz gold in 1970 to 220 oz gold in 2010. Today, the cost is 323 oz of gold.			
Postage Stamp, first class	$0.06	$0.25	$0.44	$0.49
	A pre-1965 silver dime is now worth $1.40, buying almost 3 stamps today!			
SCHOOL & ENTERTAINMENT				
College Tuition	$1,200.00	$4,757.00	$13,564.00	$26,842.00
Public School, per year	Cost in terms of gold in 1970: 33 ounces. Today, the cost is 21 ounces gold.			
College Tuition	$1,561.00	$12,910.00	$32,000.00	$35,500.00
Private School, per year	43 ounces gold for private colleges in 1970. Today, "only" 28 ounces gold.			
Movie ticket	$1.55	$4.22	$7.89	$10.50
	Movie tix are much higher than in 1970; but, if silver dimes, 1/2 as much.			
Television	$500.00	$1,250.00	$2,000.00	$2,500.00
Large, top quality	Importing foreign electronics has kept prices "down," but still 5 times higher.			
MEDICAL EXPENSES				
National Health Cost	$355.00	$2,843.00	$8,404.00	$10,920.00
Expenditure per person/year	The cost for medical care per person has ranged between 7 and 10 oz gold.			
TAXES				
Total Taxes / family of 3	$1,140.00	$4,137.00	$6,212.00	$7,440.00
Incl. Fed., State and Local	Total taxes for the average family are 6-1/2 times the amount paid in 1970.			
TRANSPORTATION				
Automobile	$3,450.00	$16,000.00	$29,217.00	$35,000.00
New, medium standard	Cost of a car varied from 9 to 35 oz gold. Today, the cost is 28 ounces gold.			
Auto Gasoline	$0.36	$1.15	$2.96	$2.50
Per gallon	Fill your tank for $7 in 1970. Today, it's $50. Or pay with two old silver dollars!			
Auto Motor Oil	$0.35	$0.85	$2.50	$4.50
Per quart	Now about 13 times as much as in 1970. Or just four old 90% silver dimes.			
Auto Tires	$13.00	$70.00	$100.00	$150.00
Each, mounted	Cost was 2 ounces gold for great set of tires in 1970; today it's less than 1 oz.			
WAGES				
Wages, average	$6,186.00	$21,027.00	$41,673.00	$50,000.00
Nationally per Soc.Sec.Admin.	8 times higher now. But in terms of gold, a DECLINE from 172 oz to 40 oz.			

Price History, Notes, Assumptions, and Attributions:

1. Precious metals prices for 1970, 1990, and 2010 are the averages of the London P.M. Fixings for Gold and Silver in U.S. Dollars. The precious metals prices shown for 2020 are based on an expectation of continued inflation of the money supply and resulting "price inflation." The calculations for the number of ounces of gold or silver needed to pay for items are based on the precious metals prices for those years compared to the item price for the specific years, using the August, 2017 gold price of $1,290 and silver at $17.00 per ounce.

2. Item prices for 2017 were as of July-August, 2017, based on extensive search of newspaper advertisements, store visits, from the internet and personal interviews. Wage amounts are from the Social Security Administration. New home sale prices are per the Federal Reserve Bank of St. Louis. Some of the data came from www.thepeoplehistory.com and from Macrotrends.

3. We have used many reports comparing costs over the decades. With a few gaps in the data, we had to estimate some prices. Overall, while we cannot prove many of the amounts, we have done our best to provide the most accurate information.

4. Special thanks to Steve Entin, Senior Fellow at the Tax Foundation, for his research on Total Taxes. He assumed a married couple with one child eligible for child credits in applicable years. Income each year is assumed to be entirely wage income, at the average economy-wide wage earnings for the year. The family is assumed to use the standard deduction. An estimate for state and local taxes was derived using the ratio of total state and local taxes deemed to be all on individuals (personal income taxes, taxes on residential property, and sales taxes) to total federal income taxes for the year, times the family's federal income tax.

5. Pre-1965 U.S. Dimes, quarters half-dollars, and dollars: A "full bag" is defined as $1,000 face value, either 10,000 dimes, 4,000 quarters, 2,000 half-dollars, or 1,000 dollars. When newly minted, a full "bag" of dimes, quarters and halves contained 720 ounces of pure silver. However, dealers typically use 715 when calculating the value of a "bag" because there has been surface wear from circulation. Example: $1,000 face in old circulated dimes contains roughly 715 ounces of pure silver if you melted the 10,000 coins. Therefore, we have used the following to calculate values in the research above: an old dime contains approximately 0.0715 oz silver; a quarter contains 0.17875 oz silver; a 50 cent piece contains 0.3573 oz silver. Silver dollars contain more silver than the comparable face value in dimes, quarters, or halves. An uncirculated pre-1936 silver dollar contains

0.77344 oz Silver. Dealers typically consider a "bag" of circulated dollars to contain 765 oz of pure silver.

6. We expect gold and silver to break out of the current sideways levels to much higher prices in 2018 and beyond. These expectations are based on unavoidable strains on financial markets due to unsustainable debt levels and the move worldwide to replace the dollar as the "reserve currency." A financial collapse worse than 2008 is expected, resulting in a world-wide "re-set." The result will be much higher prices of goods and services. We project a dramatic increase in inflation, possibly as high as 15% to 20% in 2018-2020.

Visit RhynesGuide.com to:

- *Setup a FREE 30-minute*
- *consultation with Craig Rhyne*
- *Signup for insightful e-newsletters*
- *Order more books*
- *Access video reports*
- *Live chat: (206) 719-6368*

D. Emergency kits, food reserves, "bug-out" kits, emergency power and water storage, etc.

1. If there were a natural or man-made disaster, you would want your important patient information and other pertinent data in a packet that you could quickly grab and go. The **GO|STAY|KIT** was founded in 2009. Initially called "The Ready Book," the name has been changed to reflect its use, both as an Evacuation "Go" Kit and an Emergency "Stay" Kit. To order, go to www.GoStayKit.org or Amazon.com.

2. **American Preparedness** has manufactured emergency preparedness kits for government, businesses, and national disaster relief organizations for more than 38 years. They offer many emergency kits and supplies, including Disaster Shelter Kits (that include hard-hat, flashlight, radio, short-term food and water). They carry several First Aid kits and much more. They will give you a 10% discount if you simply use code "WGE" with the salesperson at (888) 431-4511. Or if you order online, enter the WGE code at check-out on their website: www.AmericanPreparedness.com

3. Additionally, you should have at least a 3-month supply of food and water to protect your family in an emergency. We have researched this market and found an excellent company that offers many products, including food reserves (of various types and sizes), "bug-out kits," survival seeds, emergency power systems, water storage systems, and much more. The company, **Legacy Food Reserves**, is located in Salt Lake City, Utah and has a great track record of excellent prices and quick delivery. We have made arrangements for our clients and readers to get a 10% discount on all their products. You can order by calling (888) 543-7345 or go to their website www.legacyfoodstorage.com. Be sure to tell them you (on the phone or when you checkout online) that you want the 10% discount and provide the code: "WGE"

E. Storing Precious Metals and Valuables

When you own gold, silver, platinum or palladium coins or bars, you want easy access to all or most of them. You don't want to rely solely on an organization that may be located across the country and be at their mercy. And you do not want to have your metals stored in a bank safe deposit box that the government could control. Having coins and bars in your "hot little hands" means that you could readily access them to trade in a barter situation. This is not possible with physical metals held in IRA accounts; however, it is better to have physical gold, silver and platinum coins or bars in an IRA rather than "paper assets." And to get the tax advantages of an IRA, you have to give up on taking possession of the coins and have them stored by the trustee with a custodian in Delaware or Salt Lake City, for example. Note, however, that some people cash out their IRA accounts, then go ahead and pay the income taxes and 10% early cash-out IRS penalty that year. Subsequently, they use the proceeds to buy coins and take possession of them.

In most cases, you should have some "barter" coins at your home. Pick out some handy, yet hidden locations for some pre-1965 U.S. silver dimes, quarters or half-dollars, which are 90% pure silver and come in heavy canvas bags. [A full "bag" fills up a very large coffee can. I sell the full bags - $1,000 face value - in two half-bags that weigh about 27 pounds each. Smaller sizes are available.] Another excellent option for silver is the 1 oz. pure silver U.S. Eagle coins, which come in tubes of 20 each. Or Canadian Silver Maple Leafs. If you buy a complete vinyl "monster box" of 500, the box of silver Eagles contains 25 tubes of 20, with the coins protected in a stackable box that measures 4.5" high x 8.25" wide x 14" long.

For pictures of various sized portfolios and the space required, with estimated measurements, go to the Model Portfolios page of my website: www.WashingtonGoldExchange.com.

Some possible locations are: 1) Under tire chains in the garage (seriously); 2) Sealed in plastic containers, then – possibly - in a 5-gallon paint can (or similar metal container) and buried under the foundation of your house, outbuilding, dog kennel or barn; 3) Under the baseboard (eg, build a hidden drawer) in your kitchen or in a room in a discreet area; and 4) In a secret room created in your home out of dead space with false bottoms / false walls; 5) Large, heavy safes / vaults in concrete that cannot be carried off; and 6) Floor safes, possibly under your clothes dryer, preferably secured in cement. Include emergency food and water storage while you are at it.

Note that the Container Store has 30 locations all over the U.S., and it carries many plastic containers that are water-tight and in various sizes for storing valuables, including gold, silver, platinum and food. Their website is: www.containerstore.com For example, pictured below is a large, heavy-duty, screw-top seal storage unit (14" X 14" at base, 19" high):

After you have some coins / bars stored VERY close to you (at home), consider storing some at one or two additional locations away from your home. For one location, you can rent a safe deposit box at your local bank, but I discourage this. Keep in mind that the government could close the banks in desperation and limit your access or confiscate your gold.

A much better option is a non-bank, private and secure storage facility. We are fortunate to have one in Bellevue, Washington, by the name of The Safe Deposit Center. Address: 12000 NE 8th Street, Suite 100, ↄ. Citizen

Bellevue, WA 98005 Phone: (425) 455-8333. (In fact, I often meet with clients in one of their private rooms, or to make deliveries, by appointment only.) The facility is very large and can accommodate your gold, silver and platinum coins or bars, as well as large art pieces, statues, and other large items. The building is built into a hill (with offices for other businesses on the top and the secure storage boxes in a highly secure part of a massive concrete structure that seems impenetrable). They have Swiss-made safe deposit boxes / hardware and a high-tech electronic access system with interlocking entrance and exit door chambers. The facility has 2,000 boxes of various sizes, video surveillance, four private viewing rooms and 15" thick concrete walls that enclose several rows of boxes. The quarterly rental fees start at $44 (5"H x 10"W x 18"D) and go up to $600 (50"H x 22"D x 36"D). They also have the capability to rent boxes anonymously for an additional $100. Note: You can easily store a large dollar amount of gold or platinum in the smallest box; silver requires more room. Access: Check to see the hours of operation for access to your box. Insurance: It may be possible to get insurance through your own carrier.

There are many other private safe deposit / secure storage facilities (that are not controlled by the banks / FDIC) located all over the United States, many with the capability of providing secure storage with anonymity. Without attesting to their overall security, here are several: Safe Deposit Center, 12000 NE 8th St., #100, Bellevue, WA; Phone (425) 455-8333. Website: http://www.safedepositcenterwa.com

Others: Delaware Depository (Wilmington, DE); International Depository Services (IDS) of Delaware (Newcastle); IDS of Texas (Dallas); IDS of Canada (Mississauga, Ontario); Safe Deposit Center LLC in Honolulu, HI; 24/7 Private Vaults and Inwood Security Vaults in Dallas, TX; Los Altos Vault, Los Altos, CA;

Charter Private Safe Deposit, Princeton, NJ; American Guardian, Las Vegas; Florida Intervault, Fort Lauderdale; The Vaults, Las Vegas, NV; Security Center, New Orleans, LA; and Safe Haven Private Vaults, Sandy, UT.

Note: Please let me know of additional companies / locations and your impressions of their service and safety so I can update this list from time to time.

F. Recommended Books

100 Deadly Skills, Survival Edition, Clint Emerson, Touchstone, 2016.

Bug Out Bag, Your 72-Hour Disaster Survival Kit, Creek Stewart, Better Way Books, 2012.

Complete Idiot's Guide to Barter and Trade Exchanges, Jerry Howell and Tom Chmielewski, Penguin Books, 2009.

First Aid - Fundamentals for Survival, James Hubbard, Living Ready Books, 2013.

Food Storage for Self-Sufficiency and Survival, Angela Paskett, Living Ready Books, 2014.

Hawke's Special Forces Survival Handbook, Mykel Hawke, Running Press Book Publishers, 2011.

Hiker's Guide to Washington (or comparable one for your state, if available), Ron Adkison, Falcon Publishing, 1995.

Home Survivalist's Handbook (short-term apartment / suburban living), C. Eastin & R. Acker, Survival Press, 2011.

How to Stay Alive in the Woods, Bradford Angier, Black Dog & Leventhal Publishers, 2014.

How to Survive Anything - from Animal Attacks to the End of the World, Tim MacWelch, Weldon Owen, 2015.

How to Survive the End of the World as We Know It, James Wesley, Rawles, Plume (Penguin), 2009.

Hyperinflation Survival Guide: Strategies for American Businesses, Dr. Gerald Swanson, H. Figgie Publications, 2003.

One Nation, Under Surveillance, Privacy from the Watchful Eye, Boston T. Party, Javelin Press, 2009.

Prepare Your Family for Survival, Linda Loosli, Page Street Publishing, 2015.

Prepper's Long-Term Survival Guide, Jim Cobb, Ulysses Press, 2014.

Prepper's Pocket Guide, Bernie Carr, Ulysses Press, 2011.

Prepping Supplies, Patty Hahne, Skyhorse Publishing, 2016.

Prepper's Water Survival Guide, Daisy Luther, Ulysses Press, 2015.

Safe House Survival: Step-by-Step Beginner's Guide on How to Build, Stockpile, and Maintain, Ronald Williams, Kindle, 2017.

SAS Survival Guide: How to Survive in the Wild, on Land, or Sea, John Wiseman, William Morrow Paperbacks, 2015.

SAS Survival Handbook, 3rd Edition: Ultimate Guide to Surviving Anywhere, John Wiseman, William Morrow Paperbacks, 2014.

Soldier of Fortune, Guide to Surviving the Apocalypse, N.E. MacDougald, Skyhorse Publishing, 2013.

Survival Field Manual, U.S. Dept. of Defense, FM 21-76 (or updated FM 3-05.70), Pacific Publishing Studio, 2011.

Survive, Les Stroud, HarperCollins, 2008.

Survival Safe House: How to Build, Stock and Manage a Secure Survival Shelter in Your Home, Bartholomew Rommel, Kindle, 2016.

Spy Secrets That Can Save Your Life, Jason Hanson, Tarcher Perigee, 2015.

Survival, a Prepper's Guide to Life After the Crash, Steve Mattoon, Skyhorse Publishing, 2016.

Tools for Survival, James Wesley, Rawles, Plume Book, 2015.

Ultimate Survival Medicine Guide, Joseph Alton, MD and Amy Alton, ARNP, Skyhorse Publishing, 2015.

You Can Survive the Very Worst Manmade and Natural Disasters, Duncan Long, Duncan Long Publications, 2016.

G. Recommended Websites / Blogs

There are many helpful websites and blogs on the internet. Below is a partial list.

Gold, Silver and Platinum Model Portfolios:
www.WashingtonGoldExchange.com/model-portfolios/

Gold, Silver, Platinum, and Palladium current spot prices:
www.WashingtonGoldExchange.com

News / Interviews from alternate, pro free-market sources:

Economics of inflation articles by Robert Sennholz:
www.inflationomics.com

King World News (Eric King, many interviews with economists, focusing on geopolitical events, gold):
www.kingworldnews.com

Daily news - politics, economics worldwide by ZeroHedge:
www.zerohedge.com

Survival Blogs - list of the top 50 on this website:
http://www.survivaltop50.com/

Retreat Building and Preparation:
www.skilledsurvival.com/survival-retreat

"Weights, Measures and Balancing Scales," history of money by Denise Rhyne at her website:
www.youshouldbuygold.com/2011/07/
weights-measures- and-balancing-scales/

"What you Probably Didn't Learn in School about History & Law, Silver & Gold, Economics & Power, Education, and Theology," by Denise Rhyne, 2017. Go to her website:
www.YouShouldBuyGold.com (click on Menubar topics)

Visit RhynesGuide.com to:

- *Setup a FREE 30-minute consultation with Craig Rhyne*
- *Sign up for monthly e-newsletters*
- *Order more books*
- *Access video reports*
- *Live chat: (206) 719-6368*

H. Weights, Measurements, Conversions

Precious metals are quoted in Troy Ounces.

1 Troy Ounce	31.1035 Grams
1 Troy Ounce	20 dwt (Pennyweights)
12 Troy Ounces	1 Troy Pound
14.5833 Troy Oz.	1 Avoirdupois Pound (regular pound)
16 (Avoir./reg.) Oz.	1 Avoirdupois Pound
0.9114 Troy Ounce	1 Avoirdupois Ounce (regular ounce)
32.151 Troy Ounces	1 Kilogram
1 Gram	5.0 Carats
1 Gram	0.643 dwt (Pennyweight)
1.552 Grams	1 dwt
28.3495 Grams	1 Avoirdupois Ounce (regular ounce)
1,000 Grams	1 Kilogram
240 dwt	1 Troy Pound
643.01 dwt	1 Kilogram
18.2291 dwt	1 Avoirdupois Ounce (regular ounce)
291.666 dwt	1 Avoirdupois Pound (regular pound)
1 Kilogram	2.68 Troy Pounds
1 Kilogram	35.2740 Avoirdupois Ounces
1 Kilogram	2.2046 Avoirdupois Pounds
Metric Ton	1,000 Kilograms (2,204.6 pounds)
Avoirdupois Ton	2,000 pounds (907.18 Kilogram)
1 Millimeter	.0394 Inch
1 Centimeter	10 Millimeters (.0325 foot)
1 Inch	25.40 Millimeters (2.54 Centimeters)
1 Foot	12 Inches (30.48 Centimeters)
1 Yard	3 Feet (36 Inches or .91 Meter)

1 Meter	100 Centimeters (1,000 Millimeters)
1 Furlong	660 Feet or 201.12 Meters
1 Kilometer	1,000 Meters (.6214 Mile or 3,281 Feet)
1 Mile	1,760 yards (5,280 feet or 1.6 Kilometer)

Volume and Equivalents

(Liquids are slightly heavier than dry amounts in same volume.)

1/8 teaspoon (tsp)	.5 Milliliter (ml)
1/4 teaspoon	1 Milliliter
1/2 teaspoon	2 Milliliters
3/4 teaspoon	4 Milliliters
1 teaspoon	5 Milliliters
1 tablespoon - TBSP	3 teaspoons or 1/2 oz. (15 Milliliter)
2 tablespoons	1 Fluid Ounce (30 Milliliters)
1/4 cup	2 Fluid Ounces (60 Milliliters)
1/3 cup	2.64 Fl. Ounces (79 Milliliters)
1/2 cup	4 Fluid Ounces (125 Milliliters)
2/3 cup	5.28 Fl. Ounces (158 Milliliters)
3/4 cup	6 Fl. Ounces (177 Milliliters)
1 cup	8 Fl. Ounces (250 Milliliters)
2 cups or 1 pint	16 Fl. Ounces (500 Milliliters)
4 cups or 1 quart	32 Fl. Ounces (1 Liter)
1/2 gallon (2 quarts)	64 Fl. Ounces (2 Liters)
1 gallon or 4 quarts	128 Fl. Ounces (4 Liters)

Dry Measure Equivalents

3 teaspoons	1 tablespoon	.5 oz (14.3 grams)
2 tablespoons (TBSP)	1/8 cup	1 oz (28.3 Grams)
4 tablespoons (TBSP)	1/4 cup	2 oz (56.7 Grams)
5-1/3 TBSP	1/3 cup	2.6 oz (75.6 Grams)
8 TBSP	1/2 cup	4 oz (113.4 Grams)
12 TBSP	3/4 cup	.375 pound (170 Gm)
32 TBSP	2 cups	16 oz (1 pound)
4 cups	1 quart	1 Liter
1 gallon	4 quarts	16 cups
1 bushel	8 gallons	32 quarts

Fineness / Karat Gold Values

Fineness	Karat	Description
.333	8K	33.3% pure
.416	10K	41.6% pure
.500	12K	50% pure
.583	14K	58.3% pure
.666	16K	66.6% pure
.750	18K	75% pure
.833	20K	83.3% pure
.900	21.6K	90% pure
.916	22K	91.6% pure
1.000 (100%)	24K	100% pure

Temperatures / Conversion Formula

Fahrenheit to Celsius (°F to °C): First deduct 32,
then multiply that amount by 5, then divide by 9.

Celsius to Fahrenheit (°C to °F): Multiply Celsius amount by 9, then divide
that amount by 5, then add 32.

°C	°F	Description
180	356	"Moderate" Oven Temperature
100	212	Water Boils
49	120	Bacteria killed in Food; but cook ground beef, chicken, and pork to 160°F
40	104	Hot Bath
37	98.6	Body Temperature
30	86	Beach Weather
21	70	Room Temperature
5	40	Refrigerator Temperature (maximum)
0	32	Freezing Point of Water
-18	0	Freezer Temp. / Engine Oil Freezes
-10	15	Diesel Gels Without Additive
-45	-49	Freezing Point of Gasoline (average)

I. Coin Grading / Conditions

Modern bullion coins are usually free of scratches because they have not been in circulation. Some are pure gold and do not have copper to harden them, such as the Canadian Maple Leaf, Austrian Philharmonics and Australian Kangaroos, are sold in protective plastic holders / tubes / vinyl sleeves.

The American Numismatic Association adopted a 70-point system to standardize grading in 1977. This system has facilitated doing business very efficiently where grades can be relied upon. (Note the numbers in the coin grades below; the grading services get even more specific with numbers between 1 and 70.)

Certified coins: Over the last 45 years, four third-party grading services have distinguished themselves and improved business practices for dealers and consumers. They are ANACS, ICG (Independent Coin Graders), NGC (Numismatic Guaranty Corporation), and PCGS (Professional Coin Grading Service). Coins graded by these services are "slabbed" with the coin inside a hermetically sealed plastic container that must be broken to open. Certification is appropriate for numismatic (rare) coins that carry high premiums rather than "bullion coins," since it provides independent evaluation, but at a cost.

Proof A specially made coin distinguished by sharpness of detail and usually with a brilliant mirror-like surface. Proof refers to the method of manufacture and is not a condition, but normally the term implies perfect mint state unless otherwise noted and graded as below.

Mint State The terms Mint State (MS) and Uncirculated (Unc.) are used interchangeably to describe coins showing no trace of wear. Such coins vary to some degree because of blemishes, toning or slight imperfections as described below.

MS-70 Mint state 70 is a perfect coin showing no trace of wear or scratches. The finest quality possible with no evidence of contact with other coins. Very few regular issue coins are ever found in this condition.

MS-69 to MS60 Since MS-70 is perfect, there are an increasing number of fine scratches, toning variances, and evidences of contact with coins as you go down to MS-60. MS-60 coins are also known as "commercial uncirculated"/ "UNC" coins and while they are uncirculated they still have many obvious scratches and less appeal the lower the number. MS65 coins are often referred to as "Choice Uncirculated," with MS63 and MS67 slightly lower or higher grades of preservation and luster.

Almost Uncirculated (AU-50): Coins graded "AU" have only light wear on the high points, but the design details are very sharp. At least half of the mint luster is still present.

Choice Extra Fine (EF-45): Light overall wear shows on the highest points. All design details are sharp. Some mint luster is present.

Extremely Fine (EF-40): The design is lightly worn throughout, but all features are fairly sharp. Traces of luster may show.

Very Fine (VF-20 to 30): Light even wear on the surface and the highest parts of the design. All lettering and major features are readable.

Fine (F-12): Moderate to considerable, but even wear. The entire design is distinct and fairly good.

Very Good (VG-8): Well worn with main features clear, although rather flat in appearance.

Good (G-4): Heavily worn with visible design but faint in some areas.

About Good (AG-3): Very heavily worn with some portions of the lettering, date and legends worn smooth. The date may be barely or not readable.

Damaged coins: Bent, badly scratched, corroded, holed, nicked, or otherwise mutilated coins usually sell for just their "melt value" or even less.

$1 Million in gold, silver and platinum purchased 9/10/2015. Up 18.95% two years later, to $1,189,574. The yellow and green are "monster boxes," which contain tubes of 1 oz Silver Maple Leafs or American Silver Eagles. See Model Precious Metals Portfolios in Appendix B.

J. Glossary of Terms

Alloy The metal that is mixed with precious metal to harden a coin so it will last longer in circulation. Gold is frequently alloyed with copper, such as most of the American Eagle bullion coins and the old U.S. gold pieces, which are 900 fine. Note that even though the gold is alloyed with copper, such as with the American Eagle, these coins weigh <u>more</u> than the stated gold content to ensure investors get the full amount of gold. For example, the total weight of the "1 oz Gold American Eagle" actually weighs 1.0910 Troy oz, with the actual gold content exactly one ounce.

Ask Price The price that a seller is willing to take in order to make the sale.

Ag The scientific symbol for silver on the periodic chart of elements.

Assay A precise analytic test to ascertain the fineness (purity) and weight of a coin or bar of metal.

Au The scientific symbol for gold on the periodic chart of elements.

Bag Marks Minor abrasions on coins caused by their contact with other coins in a canvas bag.

Base Price The manufacturer / refinery's price for unfinished products based on the current cash commodity futures market.

Bid Price The price a buyer is willing to pay you if you want to sell to him.

Bullion Precious metal in negotiable / tradable form, such as an ingot or bar.

Bullion Coin A coin that has been minted primarily as an investment in the precious metal, usually modern issues such as the American Eagle or Canadian Maple Leaf coins.

<u>Business Strike</u> A coin which has been struck for circulation.

<u>Coin</u> A round, stamped piece of metal usually reserved for those minted by an authority that guarantees its weight and purity - most often by a government or bank - with legal tender status. (See Rounds below.)

<u>COMEX</u> The Commodity Exchange, Inc. in New York, where gold and silver, as well as many other commodities, are traded on a daily basis, usually via "futures contracts."

<u>Counterfeit</u> A reproduction of a coin by someone other than the government authorized to do so. In most cases, where the precious metals content is fine but the counterfeiter creates a fake coin that carries a high numismatic premium that he wants to profit from.

<u>Deliverable Bar</u> A precious metal bar with a weight and fineness that meets the standards required by one or more of the commodity exchanges.

<u>Depository</u> A facility where one can store precious metals coins, bars or other things. Most are privately owned and they vary as to whether they are acceptable to various trustees / organizations.

<u>ETF (Exchange Traded Fund)</u> An ETF is a security that tracks and index and represents a basket of stocks or physical holdings of commodities, but it trades like a stock on an exchange with daily price fluctuations.

<u>Fabricated Price</u> The price for precious metals in various forms (bars, grain, sponge) that are sold to industrial consumers, such as companies that make catalytic converters for automobile exhaust systems which use platinum.

<u>Face Value</u> The official currency issue value when issued. For example, a pre-1965 U.S. quarter has a face value of 25 cents; however, its real value is tied to the price of silver. The face value of a new 1 oz Gold

American Eagle is $50, but the real value / price is tied to the price of gold.

Fineness or Fine The portion of the coin or bar that is absolutely pure relative to the base or alloy. For example, American Eagle gold coins are .900 fine, meaning that 900 out of 1,000 parts are pure gold and the rest is alloy (copper). 24K = .999 fine; see Appendix H.

Fine Weight The actual weight of the pure precious metal in the bar, ingot, round or coin as opposed to the total gross weight (that include the alloy).

Gram The basic unit of weight in the metric system (31.1035 grams per Troy ounce). See more units of weight and measurement in Appendix H.

Hallmark The imprinted mark or marks on bars or ingots of precious metal indicating the manufacturer and fineness.

Industrial Price The manufacturer's (mint or refinery) final price that includes the manufacturing cost to create uniformly sized coins or bars that are desired by investors.

Ingot Usually refers to an oblong or rectangular bar.

Intrinsic Value The actual value of the precious metal content of a coin based on current prices.

London Fix The price established by the largest precious metals companies, usually twice per normal business day, used as a benchmark.

Medallion A privately issued small round, usually of precious metal but not "official coin of the realm" from a government.

Mint Luster The sheen or "bloom" on the surface of a coin resulting from the centrifugal flow of metal caused by the striking of the dies under tons of pressure. Usually frosty on business strikes as opposed to mirror-like on proofs.

Mint Marks Letters, symbols or hallmarks found on coins that indicate the mint facility where it was struck. In the U.S., P or none (Philadelphia), D (Denver), S (San Francisco), or W (West Point) have been used.

Modern Issues Coins struck for current issue, either for collectors, investors or circulation as currency.

NYMEX The world's largest physical commodity futures exchange. Trading is conducted through two divisions, the NYMEX Division (home to the energy, platinum and palladium markets); and the COMEX Division, on which all other metals trade.

Obverse The side of a coin bearing the principal design, head or device. (The opposite side is the reverse.)

Ounce When dealing with precious metals, most assume "ounce" to mean "Troy Ounce," with 1 Troy Ounce equal to 1/12 of a Troy Pound. When referring to a "regular" ounce, such an ounce is 1/16 of an Avoirdupois pound. See details in Appendix H.

Pd The scientific symbol for Palladium on the periodic chart of elements.

Pt The scientific symbol for Platinum.

Poured vs. Pressed Bar A poured bar is made by pouring molten metal into a mold (also called a "cast") to form a desired shape. Mints that make pressed bars start with what are known as "blanks." The blanks are then loaded into a machine that applies thousands of pounds of pressure with a die containing the design. Pressed bars have more intricate designs and a high-gloss finish.

Premium Generally, the amount of the wholesale / distributor markup above the intrinsic value of the coin or bar based on supply and demand.

For example, the premium on a 1 ounce Silver American Eagle may be $2 per coin, covering the cost to mint the coin and to distribute it to dealers.

Restrike A coin re-issued by a sovereign government using the original dies at a later date. An example is the Mexican 50 Peso (Centenario) issued in 1947, but still being minted with the old date.

Reverse The side of a coin opposite to the side that features the head or principal figure (the obverse).

Round Generally refers to coin-like, private company issued form of precious metals in various sizes, but not official legal tender of a country.

Spot Price The benchmark price for a large, deliverable bar of precious metal per the major exchanges / distributors. In the case of gold, a 100 oz bar; for silver, (5) 1,000 ounce bars. The spot price does not include shipping, delivery, insurance or commission. Coins and bars usually sell at a premium of at least five percent more than the spot price of the metal because of manufacturing and distribution costs, generally, the economies of scale.

Spread The difference between the Bid Price (what a dealer will pay if you sell to them) and the Ask Price (what a dealer will charge if you buy from them). The spread is usually bigger with silver than with gold; it is a bigger with smaller coins and bars and less commonly known items. Example of spread: If a dealer is buying 1 oz Gold American Eagles from the public for $1,330 per coin while selling them for $1,386, the "spread" is $56, which is the difference between the two prices. In this case, the $56 spread in terms of percentages is a "4% spread," which is how much gold would have to rise before "breaking even."

Contact Information

You can call our 24-Hour Hotline and leave a message
for Craig Rhyne by dialing (425) 522-3680
Email: craig@washingtongoldexchange.com.
Mailing Address: Washington Gold Exchange LLC
P.O. Box 368, Bellevue, WA 98009
Websites: WashingtonGoldExchange.com
and YouShouldBuyGold.com.

Visit RhynesGuide.com to:

- *Setup a FREE 30-minute*
- *consultation with Craig Rhyne*
- *Signup for insightful e-newsletters*
- *Order more books*
- *Access video reports*
- *Live chat: (206) 719-6368*

Made in the USA
Lexington, KY
25 January 2018